FRONTIERS
Essays and Writings on Racism and Culture

OTHER BOOKS BY M. NOURBESE PHILIP

Looking for Livingstone: An Odyssey of Silence
She Tries Her Tongue; Her Silence Softly Breaks
Harriet's Daughter
Salmon Courage
Thorns

FRONTIERS

selected
essays
and
writings
on
racism
and
culture
1984 – 1992

M. Nourbese Philip

The Mercury Press

The publisher gratefully acknowledges the financial assistance of the Canada Council
and the Ontario Arts Council as well as that of the Ontario Ministry of Culture and
Communications through the Ontario Publishing Centre and the
Multiculturalism Directorate of the Secretary of State.

Editor for the press: Beverley Daurio
Cover design: Ted Glaszewski
Cover photograph: Kevin Omura
Author photograph: David Laurence

Typeset in Goudy Old Style and Gill Sans by TASK.
Printed and bound in Canada.

Canadian Cataloguing in Publication:

Philip, Marlene Nourbese
Frontiers : essays and writings on racism and culture
ISBN 0-920544-90-8
1. Mass media and race relations - Canada.
2. Mass media and race relations - United States.
3. Racism - Canada. 4. Racism - United States.
5. Racism in language. I. Title.

FC104.N68 1992   305.8'00971   C92-094538-4
F1035.A1N68 1992

Canadian Sales Representation: The Literary Press Group.

The Mercury Press is distributed in Canada
by General Publishing,
and in the United States
by Inland Book Company (selected titles)
and Bookslinger.

The Mercury Press
137 Birmingham Street
Stratford, Ontario
Canada N5A 2T1

For Canada,
in the effort of becoming a space
of true true be/longing

Contents

Introduction

Echoes in a Stranger Land

I have lost my place, or my place has deserted me. This may be the dilemma of the West Indian writer abroad: that he hungers for nourishment from a soil which he (as an ordinary citizen) could not at present endure. The pleasure and the paradox of my own exile is that I belong wherever I am. My role, it seems, has rather to do with time and change than with the geography of circumstances; and yet there is always an acre of ground in the New World which keeps growing echoes in my head.
— George Lamming, *The Pleasures of Exile*

They who have put out the people's eyes, reproach them of their blindness.— John Milton

THE POSITION FROM WHICH I WRITE this introduction is a hazardous and difficult one, if only because its fluidity does a disservice to the fixedness implicit in the word "position." It is, however, appropriate that I should be writing this introduction in Tobago, since this is the first and remembered place of exile. Exile— which has come to be the signature and permanent mark of the modern age.

From one exile to another, island hopping, first to Trinidad, "for an education," British and colonial, next to Jamaica for a continuation at the tertiary level, and then to a more permanent exile in North America. Only to understand, finally, that exile had begun a long long time before I left Tobago for Trinidad, a confused eight-year-old. The exile of which I speak is a much more lasting one than I had ever anticipated.

It coming right inside we house— this exile— along with "things for so" from America, pack up in a box that Tantee sending or a barrel that Cousin Pearl mailing, it coming smelling of "she gone a foreign" and strange and new, of anything that not us. And you playing with it, touching it, feeling it, putting it on— a new pair of shorts, a dress— "look what a pretty white dolly!"; it having a smell all it own— sharp, exciting, and smelling of America and it real real— this exile. Except we not knowing that is exile we smelling when excited for so, we pressing we noses against the new clothes; we not knowing that the literature and history, even the grammar we learning in school is part of the contour map in we own geography of exile.

Back then the hidden curriculum wasn't hiding so much and we growing up knowing we leaving, that nothing around we having any value and that life only beginning when we walking up the gangplank to the big-for-so ocean liner, or up the stairs to the plane that taking we away to big country. We sucking the milk of exile at we mammy bubbies, we cutting we teeth on exile— exile in the very air we breathing.

Many-faceted and many-layered, this condition of exile is the legacy of colonialism and imperialism that first exiled Africans from their ethnicity and all its expressions— language, religion, education, music, patterns of family relations— into the pale and beyond, into the nether nether land of race. From this exile there would be no relief, no recourse, no return. In predicting that the twentieth century would be the century of race, Du Bois, the African American intellectual, was uncannily prescient.

In many respects, for Africans, exile from their ethnicity has not yet been repaired. In North America and to some degree in Canada the re-forged links with that ethnicity appear to have grown stronger in recent years. Strangely enough, in the Caribbean, in these islands that are predominantly African, the links *appear* weaker, the flight from Africa manifesting itself in either a profound erasure and silencing or a submerging under a growing Americanism through the uncritical absorption of CNN news, *Santa Barbara*, *Knots Landing*, and *Dallas*. I say *appear* since the apparent absence is deceptive and is really a presence, albeit hidden.

Although presently "positioned" in the Caribbean (having been living here for the last ten months), I have for the last 25 years— almost— made Canada my "home," another word of apparent fixity yet also subject to a dangerous fluidity.

It is May, 1992, and Los Angeles burns in response to the verdict acquitting white police officers charged with assaulting an African American, Rodney King. It is May, 1992, and in a night of riots, Toronto explodes. The word "finally" lurks there, somewhere at the back of my mind. Newspaper, television and radio reports about both events have provided the backdrop, both to the writing of this introduction and to my editing the essays collected here, which were written over the last eight years— two years short of a decade. The irony does not escape me as I read my own words cautioning against just this sort of eventuality, if Canadian society failed to grapple with racism. The irony *and* the pain.

It has been a disconcerting and disturbing experience to reread my own thoughts, opinions and conclusions on the racism permeating the institutions of Canada, including cultural ones, and to reflect on how little has changed over the years. It has, therefore, not been difficult to understand how the riots in

Toronto could have happened. While the Rodney King verdict and consequent riots in Los Angeles may have been the catalyst, the ground had been well-worked in Toronto and Canada in preparation for this confrontation and outbreak of violence.

The currents of racism in Canadian society run deep, they run smooth, lulling white Canadians into a complacency that will see racism anywhere else but in Canada. Racism is as much the determining factor in the brutal and deadly confrontation between the police and African Canadians as it is in the traditional approach of arts councils and related institutions to African-based aesthetics and African Canadian artists. It still remains a difficult and sometimes impossible task to convince white Canadians of this, and often requires, as recently happened with the Stephen Lewis report, a white individual to validate what Blacks have identified for a long time.

Traditionally, however, culture has not been a significant arena of racial contestation. Education, employment, housing, and police relations have always, and for good reason, garnered most attention— political, academic, investigative, and personal. This is ironic, given that the European onslaught against Africans was as much against their culture as against their persons. The significance of the 1990 confrontation between the Royal Ontario Museum (ROM) and the African Canadian community over the display, *Into the Heart of Africa*, lay in the fact that for the first time the issue of culture as a site of contestation attracted and galvanized wide-based attention. The dismissal by white Canadians, led by the media, of the complaints by African Canadians once again underscored the resistance of Canadian society to any acknowledgement or acceptance of racism.

Having said that, however, it is only fair to acknowledge that over the eight years during which I wrote the articles, essays, and letters now comprising *Frontiers*, arts councils and cultural institutions have made some changes. Many of these do not go far enough, being still at the stage of reports on what *ought* to be done. The Canada Council, the Ontario Arts Council and the Toronto Arts Council all struck committees, ostensibly to consider how better they could serve their multi-racial and multi-ethnic communities; many arts council panels are now much more representative of these communities. In their recognition that all is not well in the cultural body of Canada, these changes represent hair-line fractures in the at times overwhelming and oppressive structures standing guard over "Canadian culture." This is the best possible interpretation of these developments; at worst, these responses may be seen as the system adapting and shifting, as systems always will, in order to remain essentially the same.

All of which brings me to the composite nature of the phrase "Canadian culture." By culture I include all its expressions, including language, religion, and education— the many ways in which a people organizes its life and living that distinguish it from any other. The devastation that capitalism wrought on the culture of Africans brought to the Caribbean and the Americas, not to mention that of the Native peoples, is illustrative of the significance, if not indispensability, of culture to human society. The intent of the onslaught against Africans was two-pronged: to achieve a cheap unwaged source of labour *and* to destroy their cultural life. The latter was not an accidental by-product of the former, but integrally linked to it; an African workforce that had no cultural base or resource to rely on would be a more pliable, less rebellious one. David Livingstone understood this when he reasoned that he first had to destroy the customs and mores of continental Africans *before* he could bring commerce and religion.[1]

There have been times when I have thought the unthinkable— that it is a less cruel act to kill a people, leaving their culture and respect for it intact, than to denude them of their culture and by various means deride and destroy it, leaving them to howl their pain and anger on down through the centuries. And isn't that partly what Los Angeles and Toronto, and before that Miami, and before that Watts, and before that the Haitian revolution and before that— have been all about? The howling of our pain and anger at the loss of our cultures.

[O]ur capacities for language, for thought, for communication, and culture— do not develop automatically in us, are not just biological functions, but are, equally, social and historical in origin... they are a *gift*— the most wonderful of gifts— from one generation to another. We see that Culture is as crucial as Nature.
— Oliver Sacks[2]

To strip a people of the gift of their culture is a double act of inhumanity— for both the victim *and* the perpetrator, who is also a victim. It becomes even more heinous for the perpetrators of this crime— Europeans and their descendants (in this case, white Americans and Canadians)— to condemn and blame the victims for their deculturation— their loss.

It is remarkable, in fact, to note how, after having had so much taken from them, having been given nothing, Africans in the New World have created so much that is new, exceptionally beautiful and indispensable to humanity: this is, in fact, an astonishing act of survival and witness to the African genius.

The Atlantic trade in Africans severed Africans in the Caribbean and the Americas from their cultural roots; the Atlantic now represents a synaptic break in the circuit of cultural continuities which run back and forth— the Yoruba drum beats crossing to Trinidad, Jamaican reggae crossing "back" to Zimbabwe and South Africa, Nzinga to Harriet Tubman and Sojourner Truth back to Winnie, Malcolm to Biko and back, and on, and on.

Having lived for the last several months in a society also split along racial lines, this time African and Asian, and one which appears to thrive on racial brinkmanship, albeit verbal, once again the significance of culture and cultural continuity becomes apparent. Although Asian indentureship was, in very many respects, very similar to from slavery, in one remarkable and significant aspect the experience of the African and Asian differed— in the permission the colonial government granted the latter to keep their language, customs, rituals and culture, although white colonial society considered these at best exotic, at worst pagan, savage or primitive. Prohibition vis-à-vis permission— these diametrically opposed attitudes sum up the difference in how the colonial powers treated these two groups. In the one case the drum, the orishas (gods)— Shango, Oshun, Yemoja and countless others— not to mention the tongue itself, would be outlawed; in the other, Hindi, Bhojpuri, the pundits, the tassa (drum) and even ganja (smoked by holy men) would be allowed. That African cultural practices have continued at all, in whatever fashion they have, is a testament to the vitality of African cultures and the will to survive.

The different treatment of these two cultures, African and Asian, has had a lasting effect on how these groups view themselves and their cultures— in one instance, to be cherished; in the other, to be ashamed of. Not only the effect on the peoples, but the difference in attitude to the two groups continues on down to the present time. It has its roots in a pernicious type of racism that ranked subject peoples, so that those whose cultures more closely approximated European culture, in having a written language and big stone buildings, were considered a cut or two above the non-literate savage living in the jungle— read African.

If there is one central point around which the essays and articles in this collection focus, it is the need on the part of what has traditionally been seen as Canadian culture, as represented by arts councils and organizations, to respect those cultures— African, Asian, and Native— that had long established circuits of culture, which Europeans interrupted, bringing with them their own cultures, with its central economic practice of capitalism. The absence of that respect— in many instances, the outright disrespect— makes itself felt all the way down from the Boards of Directors, through the panels and staff to the individual artist.

I carry a Canadian passport: I, therefore, am Canadian. How am I Canadian, though, above and beyond the narrow legalistic definition of being the bearer of a Canadian passport; and does the racism of Canadian society present an absolute barrier to those of us who are differently coloured ever belonging? Because that is, in fact, what we are speaking about— how to belong— not only in the legal and civic sense of carrying a Canadian passport, but also in another sense of feeling at "home" and at ease. It is only in belonging that we will eventually become Canadian.

How do we lose the sense of being "othered," and how does Canada begin its m/othering of us who now live here, were born here, have given birth here— all under a darker sun? Being born elsewhere, having been fashioned in a different culture, some of us may always feel "othered," but then there are those— our children, nephews, nieces, grandchildren— born here, who are as Canadian as snow and ice, and yet, merely because of their darker skins, are made to feel "othered."

A long and passionate discussion with a fellow African Caribbean Canadian (how many identities can dance on a maple leaf?), clarified some of the issues for me around belonging and becoming Canadian. Our discussion arose out of an article by Bharati Mukherjee about Salman Rushdie. In it, Mukherjee opined that, unlike in the case of the South Asians, Afro-Caribbean people in England could eventually become English because of similarity of language, religion and dress.

My friend agreed, and argued further that a similar distance and difference existed between a Northern and Southern European— a Swede and a Sicilian, for instance— as between the English and Afro-English or Afro-Saxons. By extension, the same arguments can be applied to Canada— English Canada, at least, with all its institutional and cultural replicas of England. In a letter to her that was never mailed I wrote:

We cannot, however, rely solely on dress, religion and language— even accepting that these are the same. And while they may be the same, we wear them all differently. While religion and language in the Caribbean bear the unmistakeable stamp of Christianity and England, Africa has also left her indelible mark on these. This is not the place to go into detail on the African influences on religion, but suffice it to say that the practices of Spiritual Baptists, Rasta, and pocomania, to mention but three of the many aspects of religious worship of Caribbean people, all incorporate African beliefs and practices. Not to mention orisha worship— worship of African deities— which has always been there but is rapidly growing among "Afrosporic" peoples. And wherever they have scattered, African Caribbean peoples have taken these forms of worship with them. In the heart of Toronto, I have seen Africa in the ceremony of worship in a tiny Spiritual Baptist Church. The Caribbean demotic, as well, is as much the linguistic descendant of Africa as of England. As Rex Nettleford[3] has argued, Europe may have governed, but Africa ruled.

The perceptions and attitudes of the dominant society, however, must also be taken into account in the dynamics of belonging and becoming. And there is nothing in either English or Canadian society that suggests that African people are particularly welcome by the host society. From the establishment— location and number— of immigration offices overseas, to the policing of Black people domestically, including their difficulty in obtaining adequate employment, housing and education, the evidence of the lack of welcome, if not open hostility, is there. From the point of view of white Canadian and English people, the distance between African peoples and themselves is infinite, not infinitesimal as Mukherjee would have us believe, and they wish to keep it that way.

It matters not a jot that an African Canadian person may think herself very much integrated within Canadian society and a part of it— they may and do wear the same clothes, attend the same churches, go to the same schools, live in the same neighbourhoods— if the dominant society continues to see them— us— as alien, different and Other, they cannot truly belong to the society. It behooves us all to remember how much an integral part of German society Jews were, prior to the rise of Nazism and Hitler. And, closer to home, those middle class Blacks who moved to the suburbs, dressing and speaking like Canadians, driving the same cars Canadians did, discovered how much and how little they belonged when the police began shooting their young in the streets like dogs. Having a house in the suburbs like all good Canadians aspire to was no protection— not if your child was Black.

It is important that we not read a culture through the eyes of the middle class, whom I believe live the same the world over— from London to Toronto, to Port of Spain to Bangkok— it matters not what country we're in. They share the same aspirations, yearn after the same material comforts— their desire— historically— in the Caribbean was to become as white and European as possible. It hasn't changed much. It is those who occupied and occupy the lower rungs of the society who have been the caretakers of Africa as it exists in the New World today— from steel pan to calypso, to reggae, to voudoun, to candomble to the very demotics that now exist.

On a lighter note, one only has to take a walk along Eglinton Avenue here in Toronto to see how we wear clothes differently— just the angle of a hat, perhaps, the slight crawl or sashay— to know that even in something as apparently superficial as dress, the continuities of style run deep.

To become unambivalently British or Canadian is to forget the history of empire that defined England, produced a Canada, and honed the beliefs and practices of white supremacy; it is to forget that our people and Europeans first met as equals— the latter being made welcome in Africa as they were here in Canada— and that the latter would use their superior technology to attempt an obliteration of African peoples and their cultures. Not to remember those things; to forget that what we now *appear* to share— education, religion, dress, legal institutions— are really tombstones erected on the graves of African customs, culture and languages, is simply to collude in our own erasure, our own obliteration.

If the individual remains *in the knowing* of what her speaking
English means, and what her worshipping an Anglo-Christian god
means in terms of her people and what has happened to them—
particularly given that the white supremacy and racism that fuelled
colonialism and imperialism are still very much alive today, this
knowledge must mediate her Englishness or Canadianness. While
the divide may appear small, it runs deep.

I seem, however, to be arguing out of both sides of my mouth—
on the one hand saying that Africans are not accepted by the
dominant culture, but also suggesting that Africans not embrace
unambivalently the dominant culture. What I am, in fact, saying, is
that the history of that lack of acceptance and rejection and hatred
is *why* we cannot unambivalently embrace the dominant culture,
and that the solution to racism and white supremacy is not
through sameness, as Mukherjee's argument seems to suggest. I
am also arguing for a subversive role for memory, that memory is
more than nostalgia— it has a potentially kinetic quality and must
impel us to action.

Should we African Canadians, therefore, turn in our pass-
ports as some have suggested, since we have shown ourselves so
ungrateful as to criticize our benefactors? We ought to leave,
some have urged politely and not so politely— the theme of
"nigger go home" is a persistent one. Those who think like this,
however, will not see such a simplistic solution. Their worst
nightmares have been and will continue to be confirmed. In the
words of my only mother tongue, the Caribbean demotic, "We
ent going nowhere. We here and is right here we staying." In
Canada. In this world so new. To criticize, needle and demand;
to work hard for; to give to; to love; to hate— for better or worse—
till death do we part. And even after— in the African tradition

of our ancestral role after death of advising and guiding our offspring— our descendants. African Canadians— Canadians.

For us Africans— the Americas and the Caribbean *were* a new world. An ocean— at times it appears an eternity— separates us from the land we came from— Africa. To reverse Blake's image of seeing an eternity in a grain of sand, at times the eternity of our separation appears a mere hop, skip and a jump away, particularly when we listen to our poets, our musicians, our artists and our griots, and witness that Africa has merely spored the New World with the genius of her sons and daughters.

The astonishing accomplishments of Africans who were freed in some instances not even 150 years ago— we are still some 46 years short of the bicentennial of the earliest emancipation date, 1838[4]— beggars the imagination. And sometimes I believe the overwhelming impediments put in our way are a back-handed compliment to our achievements and our potential. These obstacles are, in fact, partially an acknowledgement of fear on the part of the dominant white culture— the fear, *as they perceive it*, that, given half a chance, we will replace them in all fields.

However, the onslaught against Africans in this New World has not let up since the first African was brought here. At times, it appears that there is a loosening of the grip— the passing of Civil Rights legislation and the adoption of affirmative action policies in the U.S., and the adoption of human rights legislation in Canada— but, as in the last decade under Reagan, Bush, Thatcher and Mulroney, there has been more than enough reason to sit down by the rivers of Babylon and weep. Consider the plight of what is now called the Black underclass in the United States, or the African peoples of Azania; consider Haiti today— the first country in the Caribbean and the Americas to have a successful revolution led by the former African slave, Toussaint L'Ouverture; consider the shootings of Black youth and adults in Canada. Consider and consider, then consider some more.

For Africans in the Caribbean and the Americas, who in the words of the spiritual, have been trying to sing their songs in a strange land, be/longing *is* a problematic. Be/longing *anywhere*— the Caribbean, Canada, the United States, even Africa. The land, the place that was the New World was nothing but a source of anguish— how could they— we— begin to love the land, which is the first step in be/longing, when even the land was unfree? How could they— we— be/long to and in a land that was not theirs— ours— but some burgher's in Amsterdam, or London? How do you begin to be/long when everything around you conspires to keep you alien— the language, the customs, the spirituality? And yet they began— those early Africans— singing their songs in this land so new and so strange— songs that harked back to their earlier be/longing elsewhere, but in singing those songs they were making their first mark of be/longing to the land, the place— this world so new— the Caribbean and the Americas.

The only peoples who be(truly)long here— who be long here (I use "be" in the African American vernacular sense), are the Native peoples. Unlike all other peoples who came here, the African did not choose to come, but was forced to come as a consequence of one of the most cruel enterprises in history, the trans-Atlantic trade in Africans.

Five hundred years ago, Columbus came sailing into the womb— cunt if you will— that was the Caribbean, entering what was for the European a new world, sowing it with the poisoned seed of Europe to produce Old World mutations of genocide, devastation and racism. He did what Europe was going to do sooner or later— enc(o)unter the Caribbean and the Americas, and so began a 500 year experiment of testing their time-worn theories of white and racial supremacy in the laboratory of the Caribbean and the Americas, creating thereby the wound— the cut— that continues to suppurate. Womb and wound; cunt and cut— the paradigmatic axis around which the male European would move in the New World.

Five hundred years! Africans be long here now. Sometimes it appears we be too long here, but there *is* nowhere else to go. Not to Africa, not to England; not to Spain or France, but here in this world so new— the Caribbean, the Americas, including Canada— singing their songs in a stranger land— by the rivers of Babylon.

Sometimes it appears that we Africans in the New World have been weaned forever on the milk of otherness; we have been too long "othered" by those societies who traditionally have thought and currently think nothing of enriching themselves on our labour then discarding us— the detritus of capitalism. I am reminded that there was a time when it was cheaper to get rid of an African slave who was no longer useful, and buy a new one, than to continue to provide for her. Could this have been the start of the "nigger go home" attitude? We need now, however, to be m/othered by those very societies and cultures which have destroyed our cultures, enriched themselves on our exploited labour, and who would now banish, if not destroy us. By Canada. But more important than that, Canada *needs* to m/other us. Her very salvation depends on m/othering all her peoples— those who be/long(ed) here when the first Europeans arrived— the Native peoples; as well as those, like the African, who unwittingly encountered History and became seminal in its development.

How best this m/othering will be carried out is the work of educators, parents, children, business people and politicians— the entire society. But it must *not* be left up to politicians. Further, it ought not to be and cannot be accomplished by obliterating the history of the Native, the African or the Asian, and Canada's role as an abuser. That is why it is so important to keep the slash— in *all* its negative connotations— in m/othering.

We must not forget. Neither the oppressor nor the victim— not Canada or the Native person, the African or the Asian— we will not forget. As I wrote to my friend, to forget would be tantamount to engaging in massive and collective social amnesia. But since we each, individually and collectively, are equally entitled to share in this land, we had better find ways of encouraging ourselves and each other to sing our songs— in this land that, with the exception of the Native people, *is* a strange land for us all. (By behaving as if he was the only one who had a right to the land, the European even tried to make it strange for the Native person.)

We all know the alternative; we witnessed it in May, 1992, in Toronto. We will witness it again. And again. Unless all Canadians, particularly those who traditionally comprise the dominant groups— white Canadians— understand how racism fatally affects the body politic. The choice is a stark one— between a society increasingly riddled with inequities— truly a stranger land— the haves ensconced behind burglar bars, the have-nots occupying the streets in increasing numbers, and between them both the police creating a buffer zone at best, or at worst performing the functions of an occupying army on behalf of the well-to-do; and a society which becomes a "home" where all Canadians be/long.

Whichever direction we take, it behooves us to remember that "our opponents are our co-creators, for they have something to give which we have not."[5] This is the challenge facing all Canadians— African, Asian, European and Native— finding out what we can offer to and accept from each other. It is the only way we will transform this place from a stranger place to one of true be/longing.

END NOTES:

1. Tim Jeal, *David Livingstone*, Heinemann.

2. Oliver Sacks, *Seeing Voices*, Harper Perennial.

3. Former Rhodes scholar, presently a professor at the University of the West Indies, and choreographer of the National Dance Troupe of Jamaica.

4. Although England abolished slavery in all her colonies in 1834 (the earliest date of emancipation for all slaveholding nations), Africans in English colonies had to continue under an apprenticeship period for another four years until 1838.

5. Marion Milner, *Eternity's Sunrise*, Virago, 1987.

Who's Listening?

artists, audiences & language

If no one listens and cries
is it still poetry
if no one sings the note
    between the silence
if the voice doesn't founder
    on the edge of the air
is it still music
if there is no one to hear
is it love
or does the sea always roar
in the shell at the ear?[1]

MALE, WHITE AND OXFORD-EDUCATED, he stands over my right shoulder; she is old, Black and wise and stands over my left shoulder— two archetypal figures symbolizing the two traditions that permeate my work. He— we shall call him John-from-Sussex— represents the white colonial tradition, the substance of any colonial education. Abiswa, as we shall call the other figure, represents the African-Caribbean context which, as typical of any colonial education, was ignored. She is also representative of a certain collective race memory of the African.

Neither of these archetypes individually represents what I would call my ideal listener or audience. John-from-Sussex has always represented his standards as universal, but they all— with the exception of excellence which knows no race, class or gender— bore the trademark "Made in Britain." Abiswa, through an artificially imposed ignorance which I have tried to correct, I know too little of. To partake in her wisdom requires a different process from the one learnt from John-from-Sussex, demanding that one trust the body which, together with the mind, forms one intelligence. This was not what John-from-Sussex was about.

There has been a recent shift— since the completion of two manuscripts of poetry[2]— in my positioning of this audience of two: John-from-Sussex has become less substantial, more of an apparition; Abiswa has emerged even more clearly from the shadows. Bridging the split that these two archetypes represent is a difficult process: each represents what the other is not— each is, so to speak, the other's Other. A dialogue between the two is essential.

All of this may seem an unusual introduction to the issue of audience, but since I believe that each artist (*artist* here and throughout this piece is used inclusively to refer to all disciplines) has an ideal audience— made up of one or several individuals— lurking somewhere in her psyche, it seemed appropriate. These "ideal" audiences have some bearing on the real audience the artist and/or her work seeks or finds.

If we take the example given above, for instance, both John-from-Sussex and Abiswa have some rooting in a certain reality which faces me whenever I write— the need to make choices around language and place, both of which inevitably impact on audience. If I use John-from-Sussex's language will

Abiswa and her audience understand and vice versa? Which is
the more important audience? Which do I value most and from
what perspective? Will Abiswa even care to understand a piece
such as this? One audience may have more economic clout than
others, and one, certainly in my case, offers me a more profound
emotional and psychic satisfaction. And some may ask: why
choose at all— why the need to have to choose any audience?

Unless the writer creates only for herself, there comes a time
when she must become aware, however vaguely, that there exists
such an animal as an audience. It may only be an awareness that
operates at a very basic level of trying to determine who will come
out to a poetry reading, installation or display, or who will buy
books, but it begins to make itself felt. And often the artist may
only be aware of who her audience is not— often more predictable
than who it is.

Audience is a complex and difficult issue for any artist,
particularly in today's world where any sense of continuity and
community seems so difficult to develop. It becomes even more
complex for the artist in exile— working in a country not her
own, developing an audience among people who are essentially
strangers to all the traditions and continuities that helped
produce her. Scourges such as racism and sexism can also create
a profound sense of alienation, resulting in what can best be
described as psychic exile, even among those artists who are not
in physical exile. The Canadian-born Black artist, artist of colour,
or the white lesbian artist, for example, all face dilemmas over
audience similar to that of the artist who has more recently—
relatively speaking— arrived in this country.

It is as well to note that legal citizenship in no way affects
the profound and persistent alienation within a society at best
indifferent, if not hostile, to the artist's origins, her work, and

her being. Many of us, no matter how old our citizenship, remain immigrants in a profoundly psychic sense. Some of us, recognizing this, choose to emphasize that alienation— it appearing a more positive position. This choice, however, results in all sorts of contradictions when it comes to funding and meeting funding requirements. Where the immigrant worker is required to have Canadian experience, the immigrant artist must show the Canadian component in her work to qualify for funding.

Even for those who have managed to adapt to Canada, there still remains the fact that much of their work will continue to draw on the imagery, rhythms, the emotional resources developed in their countries of origin. This was how an Australian painter described the issue for her: "As an artist you use certain reference points which have a bearing in a different geographic location— unless the viewer knows what these reference points are, there is no comprehension beyond organization of the work in terms of shape, form and colour." A more blatant example of this problem lies in the different sense of colour that countries have. A Jamaican artist described to me how her colours became more muted and sombre when she painted here in Canada.

Which Canada do I speak of— the West or the East? Urban or rural Canada? These are important questions since most immigrants come to the large metropolitan areas which is where many artists attempt to carve out a niche, however uncomfortable, for themselves. My experience is with the urban East— Toronto be more specific, and is that of a Black, female writer. I do not pretend to speak for all of Canada, and only the audience of this piece will be able to judge whether my experience may be easily transferable.

I cannot and do not intend to provide any definitive answers on the issue of audience for those in exile (by exile I mean not

only those of us who have physically come to this country, but
the many, many others who count themselves in exile for any
number of reasons, in this society). I don't think there are any
definitive answers, and I am not even sure whether the questions
I pose are the right ones for anyone else but myself. What I want
to do, however, is raise the issues and questions, reveal the
contradictions as they have affected me and others like myself,
and see where, if anywhere, they take us. More than anything
else, what follows is a meditation on the issues of audience.

RECEPTION, RESPONSE, COMPLETION

ONE OF THE MOST IMPORTANT impulses in all art is, I believe, the
impulse to communicate; this in turn depends on reception and
response for completion of the work in question. The late
Raymond Williams, the Marxist critic, wrote as follows: "...in
the case of art, where simple consumption is not in question,
no work is in any full practical sense produced until it is also
received." How, then, is work from communities that appear
marginal to the mainstream, with what Williams so aptly describes as their "emergent energies" completed— that is, received
and responded to, both by audiences of the more dominant
culture, as well as audiences that comprise the artist's natural
community? A few examples will best highlight this dilemma.

   The Rez Sisters. I saw this play several months ago among a
predominantly, if not completely, white audience. Everyone
appeared to enjoy the play tremendously, yet I was uncomfortable. Uncomfortable because, although I was convinced that
what I was watching was an authentic and successful attempt to
portray one aspect of Native life on the reservation, I felt that the
audience, which was, in fact, a settler audience, was being let off

too easily. I felt that they could— I am sure they did— leave the theatre feeling that "reservation life wasn't so bad after all." Those who were feminist could comfort themselves with the remarkable strength of the women. I was equally convinced that a Native audience would complete that play in a very different way— they could and would be able to contextualize much more completely the events that played themselves out on the stage. They would not leave the theatre as comfortably, or as comforted, as did the white audience.

So too with *The Coloured Museum*, which also played to full houses of predominantly white people. Here was a powerful, painful, and at times funny collage of Black American life over the centuries. There were many scenes that were "funny" which I laughed at, my laughter always tinged with the pain represented in those opening scenes on the slave plane— a pain that circumscribes my history. Why were *they* laughing though? Were they laughing at the *same* things I was laughing at, and if their laughter lacked the same admixture of pain, was it laughter which, having been bought too cheaply, came too easily? Were they, therefore, laughing at me and not with me?

These are but two examples. There are several others that elaborate the same issue; they raise complex issues around marketing and audience. *The Coloured Museum*, for instance, was never advertised in the Black newspapers, which is where many Black people get their information about activities of interest and relevance to them. Tarragon Theatre, however, did not need to advertise in the Black press to fill its house. Do they, indeed, have an onus to do so when they are staging Black works or works that relate specifically to a particular group in society? *The Rez Sisters* played first at the Native Centre on Spadina, then returned for a run at a more mainstream theatre.

These examples raise issues applicable to all disciplines of art— even music, which appears to be the discipline that most easily crosses cultural barriers. The lyrics and music of the late Bob Marley were wrought and wrested out of the unrelenting poverty and grimness of the Trenchtown ghetto; he sang of better times for Black people, when "Babylon" would be no more. How many North Americans who "grooved" on his music cared to understand this or even cared?

It is a truism that we each complete a novel, play, poem or painting differently, depending on factors as diverse as age, gender, class, and culture. What concerns me is the ever-present danger that a white mainstream audience in Toronto is likely to come away from a play like *The Rez Sisters* or *The Coloured Museum* with none of their stereotypes shaken or disturbed, which is not necessarily the fault of the playwright. He or she may have written the play in question with a Native or Black audience in mind.

Can you ever have a valid completion of a work by an audience that is a stranger to the traditions that underpin the work? This question leads us back to that dichotomy between dominant and sub-dominant cultures— the old "mainstream versus margin" argument. The significance of this dichotomy lies in the fact that those of us who belong to those sub-dominant groups— women, Africans, peoples of the formerly colonized world— have been rigorously schooled in the traditions of the dominant cultures— European and patriarchal. This experience along with the fact that we are constantly immersed in the dominant culture of the world— still patriarchal and now American, makes it much more possible for us to receive and respond to work from these cultures, than it is or ever has been in the reverse. We are, at times, even better able to understand and respond more positively to works from the dominant culture than we do to work coming out of our own traditions— such is the pernicious effect of racism, sexism and colonialism. Could we, however, argue that education offers one solution to this problem? Possibly, but we would do well to remember that the education of colonized peoples— I include women in this group— has traditionally been closer to brainwashing than to education.

EXOTICA/NOSTALGIA

THOSE OF US FROM hot, moist parts of the world (sex-positive cultures as I have recently seen them described), who work in traditions originating in our countries of origin, face the ever-present danger that our work may be considered and categorized as "different" or "exotic." Not understanding the tradition and standards, the audience, including critics and reviewers, suspends the practice of criticism, replacing it with meaningless adjectives like "great" or "wonderful."

Another kind of reception and response is best illuminated by the following excerpt from a review of an anthology, *Other Voices: Writings by Blacks in Canada*, edited by Lorris Elliott.

European literature has benefited from Black writers such as Aesop, Pushkin and Dumas. American culture has incorporated the voices of Langston Hughes, Gwendolyn Brooks, Alice Walker, Marge Piercy, or Imamu Amiri Baraka (Leroi Jones). But Canadian Blacks, like Canadian whites, still do not know if they are coming or going with their identity problems. *Other Voices: Writings by Blacks in Canada*, edited by Lorris Elliott, is a collection of poetry, prose, and drama without any direction beyond herd instinct.
The very word "other" in the title is a dim bulb in regard to visible

minorities. It cues the reader (Black, white or other) to expect
stereotypes. That is exactly what follows. "Nigger," "fight," "pain,"
"passion," "cause," "rage," "tears": the language falls predictably
flat— though the suffering motivating the outpourings is very real.
A few entries break though the barrier of boredom to move a
heart and mind willing to open this anthology, which could have
been an important book.[3]

Apart from revealing a profound ignorance— writers like
Pushkin and Dumas did not write as Black men, but as Europeans, and to parallel their experiences with that of American Black
writers serves neither experience well— the quotation reveals the
latent racism always at work in Canada. By attempting to parallel
the experience of Canadian whites and Blacks, the reviewer seeks
to dissemble his racism: "Canadian Blacks, like Canadian
whites, still don't know if they are coming or going with their
identity problem." He exculpates, under the guise of "objective
criticism," the white Canadian audience, including critics and
reviewers like himself, for their massive failure to understand the
history and traditions of racism that would give rise to the use
of words like "nigger," "fight," and "pain."

What is, however, even more instructive of the issues I raise
in this section, is the imagery the reviewer approved of and
selected to quote as examples of the better work appearing the
anthology: from *Market in the Tropics*, "Mangoes/Tama-
rinds/...wild meat on hooks," and from *The Profile of Africa*
which "expresses the sensuous beauty of blackness" (sic), "the
beautiful, strong, exotic in profile/flowering lips/silhouette ob-
sidian planes..." These poems may very well have been the better
ones (not having read them I make no comment on them here),
but it is, in my opinion, no accident that these are the poems

and the imagery that the reviewer believes "saves the volume from being another boohoo job." The sensuous beauty of Blackness— I could write volumes on this subject— is a far more appealing image for most whites than an angry Black man or woman. While I acknowledge writing about one's anger and pain without appearing to descend into rhetoric, polemic, and cant is difficult, to dismiss the work of writers attempting to bring a long tradition of struggle against racism into literature as another "boohoo job" is racist in the extreme.

Ignorance and laziness. These are the qualities at the heart of both kinds of responses described above— the over-eager response reserved for anything in the slightest bit different or appearing exotic, or dismissal. The welcome change in the picture comes from the attempts now being made by feminist critics, some of whom have finally begun to assess critically the works of women from other traditions.

The nostalgia factor presents another conundrum for the artist in exile— particularly those, like immigrants, in physical exile. The "natural" audience for such an artist is the audience from "back home." So starved, however, is this audience for anything remotely evocative of "home," that it accepts uncritically whatever is reminiscent of it. This is what I mean by the nostalgia factor.

The need to maintain continuity and traditions is a powerful one with all groups; it is a need which is assuaged in the articulation of many mainstream art forms— the ballet, opera, Shakespearean drama. The more newly arrived (relatively speaking) are not the only ones who indulge in nostalgia.

There is, however, a danger for the artist— the danger of falling into complacency. In my case, for instance, coming from the Caribbean where the use of demotic variants of English (dialect) is widespread, use of dialect is an immediate entry into the hearts and minds of a Caribbean audience. In such a context the audience is less concerned with what the artist is doing with his or her discipline, provided the need to be reminded of "how it stay" back home is met. If the artist is content with this response, then a sort of stasis results which is fatal to any growth on her part. But audience response in this context is powerful, seductive *and* difficult to turn one's back on for the less tangible, less certain rewards of "growth" or "practising one's art seriously." I do not suggest that the last two goals are incompatible with a strong audience response— they should not be— but they often mean the audience has to do some work as well, and nostalgia appears far more compatible with entertainment rather than with art.

AUDIENCE AND LANGUAGE

THE CHOICE FACING A WRITER from Eastern Europe or Italy or Latin America is a stark one: work in your mother tongue and— at least in Canada— be restricted to an audience sharing a similar linguistic heritage, or work in English with the potential of a much wider audience— minus your natural audience.

For the writer from the English or French Caribbean, the two official languages of Canada are also their languages. English is "theoretically" as much my mother tongue as it is for a writer from London, Ontario. But we know differently, and my experience with English encompasses a very different experience from that of the English-speaking Canadian. Like the writer from Eastern Europe, we too have a nation language (dialect) which is, however, a variant of English.

The choice of language for the Caribbean writer can, there-fore, be as stark as that outlined in the first paragraph in this section. If you work entirely in nation language or the Caribbean demotic of English you do, to a large degree, restrict your audience to those familiar enough with it; if you move to standard English you lose much of that audience and, along with that loss, an understanding of many of the traditions, history, and culture which contextualize your work.

Language has been and remains— as the South African example shows— a significant and essential part of the coloniza-tion process; the choice between Caribbean demotic and stan-dard English becomes, therefore, more than choice of audience. It is a choice which often affects the choice of subject matter, the rhythms of thought patterns, and the tension within the work. It is also a choice resonant with historical and political realities *and* possibilities.

In writing correct sentences, ending words with "ing" instead of "in'" making my verbs agree with their subjects, I am choosing a certain tradition— that of John-from-Sussex. My audience, for the most part, is going to be a white audience, and possibly an educated Black Caribbean audience. However, in order to keep faith with Abiswa, I must, within my writing self, constantly subvert the tradition of John-from-Sussex. This doesn't necessar-ily enlarge my audience to include the less formally educated speakers of nation language— on the contrary it probably reduces that segment of the audience since the work becomes more "difficult." It does, however, I hope, leave whatever audience there is less complacent and less comfortable with things as they appear to be.

COMMUNITY, AUDIENCE, MARKET

RAYMOND WILLIAMS writes that

[o]ur way of seeing things is literally our way of living, the process
of communication is in fact the process of community: the sharing
of common meanings, and thence common activities and
purposes; the offering, reception and comparison of new
meanings, leading to the tensions and achievements of growth and
change.

Toronto is a city of many communities which individually
meet the above description; these communities do not, however,
make up a larger community— particularly in the arts where there
is undeniably a dominant culture— "a central system of practices,
meaning and values."

The artist has always been sustained by community even if
it was a community he or she rebelled against. Within traditional
societies there was, and is, a constant dialogue between audience
and artist. When, for instance, the African "commissioned" a
piece of sculpture from a village sculptor (usually for spiritual
reasons), he or she had a very clear idea as to what satisfied them
and what was a good piece of sculpture: they exercised aesthetic
judgements. So too in European cultures where the artist was in
dialogue with the community in terms of its traditions, they
shared or understood values, even if the understanding was but
the first step to rejection.

Within the larger grouping of community then, the artist
may find her audience where she could find a "hearing" and
with which she might be in some form of dialogue.

"Market" on the other hand suggests a role for art as a

commodity, with all the trappings of that representation we have come to expect— manipulation of the market; selling the product— art— as investment and/or fashion.

There is a certain connectedness between these three apparently disparate groupings— audience, community, market— at the centre of which is the artist. Bringing them together raises certain contradictions. Is, for instance, audience synonymous with market? Can you have an audience but lack a market? To answer that last question: as a Black writer I may have an audience for a novel about Black people— that audience being those Black people who are eager to read about themselves, as well as a growing number of whites who have begun to come to the understanding that other worlds apart from theirs exist. It is, however, clearly the opinion of publishers in Canada that there is no market for books about Black people: they believe that whites are not interested and that Blacks either do not, or are unable to, buy books. Therefore, there is no market for books about Black people. Despite the audience I may have, the perceived market forces, interpreted with a sizeable dollop of racist arguments, supersede.

That a popular art form— dub poetry— has been able to widen the audience for its poetry is, I believe, because of the welding of the Black oral and musical traditions. The strongest African art form to survive outside Africa among its scattered peoples has been its music; it has been the most pervasive and persistent. In the case of the dub poets like Linton Kwesi Johnson, one of the first proponents of this style, the poetry was written in the Jamaican demotic— patois or creole— and underscored with reggae rhythms. Canadian dub poets, also using a demotic variant of English, have not restricted themselves to these rhythms, but use a variety of others. They are essentially protest poets working in the powerful oral and musical traditions of Abiswa.

The crossover mechanism between Black and white audiences in dub, has been the music. As the earlier example of Leonard Cohen showed, music serves the function of drawing those audiences who would rather be dead than caught at a high art gathering— the poetry reading. And whether white audiences "get" the same message Blacks do from dub, is not known. (In some instances the language *must* present a barrier to complete understanding.)

That white audiences "get" something from dub is clear— one only has to look at the audiences that attend various events to know that, which may mean that the question is irrelevant. But not necessarily so, since the artist's audience does provide some challenge to the artist, if only in terms of expectations. That audiences often have a tendency to want only more of what pleased them before cannot be denied. The dub poet *may*, therefore, have to make decisions as to which traditions to emphasize— the one more familiar to Black audiences, or those with which white audiences are more comfortable. Not having discussed this particular issue with any dub poets, it may all be irrelevant to them— as an observer and writer, however, the issues present a challenge.

To say that the average size of the traditional poetry audience is small— I have counted as many as ten bodies at some of mine— is an understatement. The audience for dub poetry, however, has increased this average substantially. It is still, however, not a mass audience here in Canada— in that respect, rock and rap still reign supreme.

An artist with a market has little need for community. The reverse, however, is not as assured— the artist with both community and audience but no market will, undoubtedly, starve, unless someone supports her. The market, with its forces, can be a positive factor provided it underpins the forces created by audience and community. The market becomes a negative force when it replaces or obliterates audience and community or, even more dangerously, determines "our way of seeing things" and replaces the "process of community: the sharing of common meanings, and thence common activities and purposes" with the process of commodification.

THE AUDIENCE ON THE MARGIN

AS MENTIONED ABOVE, Toronto is a city of communities alongside the dominant Anglo-Saxon culture. Many of these communities share very little with each other except residence in the same city. Many would describe these communities as marginal to the dominant one. I have great difficulty with the concept of marginality as it is ordinarily articulated: it suggests a relationship with the dominant culture in which the marginal is considered inferior, and implies that the marginal wishes to lose its quality of marginality and be eventually absorbed by the more dominant culture.

Margin, however, has another meaning which I prefer to hold uppermost in my mind, when I work as a member of two groups— Blacks and women— traditionally described as marginal. That meaning is "frontier." Surely this meaning is encapsulated in Williams' phrase "emergent energies and experiences which stubbornly resist" the dominant culture. The concept of frontier changes our perception of ourselves and the so-called mainstream. All of which is not to deny that there is a dominant culture, with a "central system of practices, meanings and values"

(Williams). And this culture receives by far the lion's share of funding and government support. However, exploiting the other meaning of margin offers another perspective, one which challenges the old, lazy ways of thinking by which we have colluded in our own management. To twist the aphorism somewhat— marginality is in the eye of the beholder.

Many of these communities on the frontier are communities under stress. In the case of the Black community, for instance, there is always the issue of racism, as well as issues flowing from economic depression within the community. Artists with audiences within such communities often become spokespersons for the community— this is an activity very much in keeping with the role of the poet in African cultures where he (traditionally) was the voice of the community. In our more contemporary situation, the issues are many and complex: should the artist take the audience as she finds it and reflect its views and demands, or is there an obligation on the artist's part to change the audience? Is the artist sharing with or challenging the audience, or both? And what of the Canadian audience— does the artist from the community on the margin/frontier have an obligation to teach such an audience that their practices may be negatively affecting other communities? Does culture change political realities any?

In South Africa, events have rendered many of these questions irrelevant; there the African dramatist, poet, novelist, painter have all been drafted into the struggle— willingly or otherwise. Njabulo S. Ndebele, the South African writer, in an issue of *Staffrider* writes:

The matter is simple: there is a difference between art that "sells" ideas to people, and art whose ideas are embraced by the people, because they have been made to understand them through the evocation of lived experiences in all its complexities. In the former case, the readers are anonymous buyers; in the latter they are equals in the quest for truth.

These opinions offer one way of approaching the issues raised in the previous paragraph.

FEMINISM AND AUDIENCE

Cut off from his natural audience, Angueta has to imagine a public for himself, and is unsure how much he can take for granted at either the linguistic or the cultural level.
    The "pitfall" for the writer is that of becoming over-simple or over-didactic, as the writer strives to inform a foreign audience how things are in his country rather than being able to *share with them feelings about experiences that have a common base.*[4] [my emphasis]

IN MANY RESPECTS THIS QUOTATION encapsulates the issues I have attempted to explore in this piece. I stress the last phrase both because it harked back to the opinions expressed by Williams and Ndebele, and because it provides me with an entry into the issue of feminism and audience.
    There is much that I find to criticize in the articulation of Western liberal feminism: the movement has become racist and classist in its practices, although there have been some tiny tremors and even some cracks along fault lines. This is not to suggest that the movement is monolithic— quite the contrary; but its diversity and variety may be its weakness as well as its strength. It is, however, a movement which has the potential,

often unrealized, to bridge some of those gaps— race and class for instance— isolating communities and audiences. It could, in some instances, promote that "common base" through which experiences might be shared.

The common base for women is a shared history of oppression in all its varieties and forms, as well as, I hope, a shared commitment to establishing communities organized along non-patriarchal, woman-centred, non-racist principles. While wishing to avoid reductionist arguments, as well as those body-centred theories which become at times tiresome, we must acknowledge that a basic common denominator of female experience— in all cultures and in all classes— has been the fact that our bodies have achieved a universal negative significance; bodies which have become palimpsests upon which men have inscribed and reinscribed their texts.

Feminism alone, however, is not the answer: we can hardly afford to jettison theories of class analysis. With modification and development in the face of change, they continue to offer indispensable insight into the arrangements of society; we need to continue to hone our arguments and analysis of the powerful workings of racism. While it is not *the* answer, feminism could make important and significant contributions to helping to resolve some of these issues— Black and white men, for instance, are certainly not talking to each other about race and class— or anything for that matter.

Feminist communities are in many cases ad hoc, but there *is* a feminist audience and market. Thoughts of the recent Montreal Book Fair come to mind. It is a market which differs in some degree from the traditional mainstream market. It is not, in the words of Ndebele, a market selling ideas to the people but one trying to evoke the lived experiences of women. It is a market which is still plagued by racism and classism, but it is a market which has grown out of a need on the part of women to know about their selves, their histories and their futures; a need to communicate about feelings and experiences that have a *common* vis-à-vis the *same* base; as well as the need to find out about other women.

We are a long way from a true feminist community, and even further away from a true feminist culture— one that would not, as it has tended to do, emphasize one aspect (the white and middle class) of that culture, but a culture in which the word feminist is enlarged to include those groups which have, to date, been excluded. When that is accomplished— the establishment of a true feminist culture— we shall be a long way toward having audiences who are able to complete in more authentic ways, the works of artists *whatever* their background.

Working in Canada as an "Afrosporic" writer, I am very aware of the absence of a tradition of Black writing as it exists in England or the U.S. The great Canadian void either swallows you whole, or you come out the other side the stronger for it. The Black writers here are, in fact, creating a tradition which will be different from both the English and American traditions of writing and literature by Black writers. Being the trail blazer for other writers to follow has been overwhelmingly difficult and daunting, for it has often appeared that there is nothing out there. Which was an accurate observation— for a long time there *was* nothing out there. As one dub poet described it, he felt responsible for everything— not only did he create the work, but he published *and* marketed it, as well as developing an audience for it.

All artists working in the tradition of Abiswa have felt this burden— even those Black artists working more closely within the tradition of John-from-Sussex have felt it. But there are changes— the audience for newer genres like dub and hip hop are growing not only among Black people, but also among whites. These are two forms in which Abiswa's heritage can be most clearly seen and strongly felt. Subversion of the old order— which, in fact, was not order but chaos masquerading as order — and of the new old order is alive and well in Abiswa's hands— in our art, writing and music. And there *is* an audience for it.

In keeping faith with Abiswa we find that many from John-from-Sussex's audiences are deserting in droves to seek the wisdom and vitality of the former. If revenge is what is called for, this may be the best revenge; it is also a way of reconciliation between these two traditions. It is the audience which helps to mediate this process.

END NOTES:

1. Philip, M. Nourbese, "Anonymous," *Salmon Courage*, Stratford, Ontario: Williams Wallace, 1984.
2. *She Tries Her Tongue; Her Silence Softly Breaks* (awarded the 1988 Casa de las Americas prize for poetry), and *Looking for Livingstone*, Stratford, Ontario: The Mercury Press, 1991.
3. Ray Filip, *Books in Canada*, October, 1987.
4. Review of *Cuzatlan* by Manilo Angueta, *New Statesman*, Dec. 11, 1987.

Hurrying On Up

STOIC AND PHILOSOPHICAL, I could have shrugged my shoulders in response to Micheline Wandor's *On Gender and Writing* and said, "Plus ça change, plus c'est la même chose"; instead, I decided to go ethnic and cheupsed (pronounced *choops*)— one loud, loud cheups.

Pissed off and/or disgusted— with life, with circumstances, with someone, with anything— one cheupses, in the Caribbean, that is. To suck one's teeth (which describes how the sound is made) is another expression for the same sound which, heard once, is always instantly recognizable. Why, I don't know, but men seldom, if ever, cheups. Pure but intelligible sound, cheupsing is peculiar to us— it is all woman.

But back to Micheline Wandor. Informative and thought-provoking, with a range of contributions from feminist writers— male and female (predominantly female), gay and straight, and including one husband and wife tandem writing team that, strangely, speaks with one voice (his), *On Gender and Writing* covered every genre of writing— from journalism to poetry— nicely exposing the many aspects of feminist struggle in the very different worlds of writing. I recently finished this book and thoroughly enjoyed it, but— and there was a big "but"— notice-able by their absence from the contributors were Black writers and writers of colour. Conclusion? That the issues of gender and writing must be the issues of interest and concern only to white feminist writers. I know differently, so I gave one good, long, rude cheups at the omission, deliberate or otherwise, of contributors of colour from Micheline Wandor's work and penned a letter of complaint to her.

This particular work is English, but lest we think this practice— the omission and, often, obliteration of the experiences of Blacks and people of colour— is foreign to us on this side of the Atlantic, let us cross the Pond and come closer to home and to Betty Friedan. On November 7, 1985, Betty Friedan listed in the *Toronto Star* "10 things that might be done to break the blocks that seem to have stymied the women's movement in America." One would have thought— and hoped— that somewhere among those ten precepts would be mention of the necessity to confront the racism that is a cancerous sore in the already sore body politic, both north and south of the 49th parallel. And although there are many who would prefer to ignore it, pretend otherwise, or even believe in its non-existence, racism continues to plague the women's movement.

Many feminists— both big "F" and small "f" feminists, were especially thrilled at the mention of economics and the feminization of poverty, "the shameful secret... that more and more middle class women are sinking into poverty." Is it not just as, if not more, shameful a secret that Black women and women of colour continue to be disproportionately represented in the lowest social-economic classes of American and Canadian society? Silence from Betty Friedan on the subject of race as she writes of the need for the women's movement to be "reformed to handle the modern dilemmas" (of which racism is presumably not one) "that feminism has helped to create," and to her another long, angry cheups for helping to perpetuate the unmentionable— racism.

Bringing it right home to dear, old Toronto: at a recent workshop which I, along with another woman, led, and which was attended by many feminists, one of the participants asked me to recommend reading material about Black women and the issues of feminism. The question surprised me somewhat, but I was in no way prepared for the mass and collective scribbling of the names I suggested— Angela Davis, Alice Walker, Audre Lorde, Bell Hooks— nothing esoteric or recondite in that selection. However, most of the women in the workshop had not heard of, let alone read, any of these women. Another cheups?

Cheupsing is, of course, not a solution, except in so far as it prevents one from committing mayhem; in some situations it may be downright inappropriate. An agent who tried to flog a manuscript of mine in Toronto (a manuscript which naturally and daringly features Blacks), told me that the two publishers she contacted were extremely reluctant even to look at the manuscript— because of the race of the characters. It would lose them sales, they told her, and one of them only grudgingly agreed to read it, if the agent would recommend the writing.

To cheups would be to under-react; to throw paint and write anti-racist graffiti on the premises of the publishers, to over-react and be foolhardy. Somewhere between those two responses, there has to be found some potent and efficacious remedy for this demoralizing and often soul-destroying practice of racism, of which every example mentioned above is an instance. Here in Canada, even getting people to acknowledge that there *is* a problem presents a problem, but my ear pressed to the proverbial clichéd ground tells me that more and more Black women— feminists of both the big "F" and the small "f" variety— are aware of this conspiracy of silence and are beginning to make their own noises— be it cheupsing or plain ordinary growling. Between the sound (the word) and action there is sometimes a very small gap.

This column, the first in a three-issue dry run, is my attempt at helping to bridge that gap. I promise to be quite ownway (headstrong), boldface (pushy, aggressive with lots of chutzpa) and hurry-come-up (as in those oppressed who have finally managed to acquire some measure of security after generations of struggle; they are said to have hurried). Ha! there is a lot of hurrying to do.

Massa and the Provincial Kitchens

"WE HAVEN'T HAD MUCH PRACTICE living with heat in the provincial kitchens for many years." With these words, Ross McGregor (former campaign manager of the Ontario Liberals) summed up his concern with the reforms instituted by the Liberal government since its inauguration in June, 1985. Among the areas of reform he identified in his *Toronto Star* article (December 20, 1985), were housing, day care, the environment, education, agriculture, unemployed youth, and senior citizens. The "heat" generated by these reforms had, he argued, already made some groups unhappy— doctors, the foes of separate school funding, and big business unhappy with pay equity for female employees.

Many, many years ago, when I was no older than thirteen, I was fortunate enough to witness and experience truly fundamental— one could even say revolutionary— changes. Those events were to mark my political consciousness indelibly. History, of course, has a way of catching up with, often overtaking, events; what was then perceived as truly revolutionary was, later on, to reveal itself as a part of the embourgeoisement of the African and Asian populations, taking place throughout the British Empire.

To have lived through those times in Trinidad and Tobago— the early sixties— without the advantage or disadvantage of hindsight, and with expectations unbridled by experience or cynicism, was to have lived through an experience that now makes me cheups and mutter, "he ain't see nothing yet," when I read of McGregor's concerns for the effect of reforms being instituted in Ontario— and it is an honest choice of his to use the word reform, and not change.

Everyone, barring the white upper classes— and possibly a few well-to-do brown people— was happy to see the English go; everyone, African and Asian alike, who comprised the mass of labour and peasantry, was swept up in the maelstrom of change. For them, I am convinced, it was revolutionary, though it did not constitute a revolution. For the first time an African was going to head a government of African and Asian Caribbean men and women; universal adult suffrage, for a long time unattainable, was now a given; cultural expressions like the calypso and pan bands, long despised as lower class, were validated; Islam and Hinduism were recognized as national religions; education was now free and available to every child in the country. This latter change was one that struck deeply in the hearts and minds of the people, for having neither property nor money, they saw education as the *only* way to move themselves up from where they had been for so long. And over all these specific changes hung the euphoria arising from the reality of self-government and independence, eloquently summed up in one catch phrase— "Massa day done."

The empowerment that came— and comes— from joining others— often with the only thing one could still call one's own— the body; the collective anticipation of new and better things to come; the belief that life must and would improve, and that "all a we" had a part in it, were all as integral to the times as the specific changes. So must people have felt in Nicaragua when

Somoza fled, in the Philippines when they deposed Marcos, in Cuba when the long tradition of right wing dictatorship had come to an end.

The most lasting effect of the events I witnessed as a child has been the development of a world view and belief that, if only one were to struggle long and hard enough, one could and would make meaningful and radical change for the better. Events, both international and domestic, in the last few years, have challenged this belief: the election of the right wing governments of Thatcher and Reagan and, more recently, their pale shadow, Mulroney; the unrelenting attack on the peoples of Latin America and South Africa, to name but two examples; the success of Bill Bennett's government in destroying much of British Columbia's social legislation; the shift to the right in municipal politics in Toronto, particularly visible in the Toronto Board of Education— I need not continue— we can each make our own lists. I hesitate to use a word so closely associated with left values, but what we are, in fact, witnessing is a right wing revolution in political and social life.

However, when I trace the genealogy of political change more closely, I do find some small consolation. On the streets of Port of Spain, Trinidad, I witnessed what, at thirteen, appeared to be a sudden phenomenon. It was not. It was, in fact, the culmination of centuries of struggle, beginning with the first Native person who resisted the Spaniards; taken up next by the first African slave who drowned herself rather than go into slavery; then by those African slaves who rebelled, and yet again by those Africans and Asians who, in the face of racism and colonialism, managed to get an education, turned on their collective head the Westminster rules and said to the British— "Massa day done"; and next by those individuals who, in 1970, took to the hills in

Trinidad to rebel against the very ones who had wrested power from England— the struggle is by no means finished.

Political change for the better seldom proceeds unabated, unchecked, or in one unbroken line— the late seventies and more so the eighties bear grim testimony to the reality that, as often as not, political change occurs for the worse as for the better. What my early experiences in Trinidad have done is convince me that one can change the odds.

Here in Ontario, life under the Conservative government was one marked by stagnation, hence the concern with what appears to be a plethora of change. Until such time, however, as the Liberal government begins to make fundamental changes to a system that favours capital over people, the Ross McGregors of Ontario need not worry: the "heat" in the provincial kitchens— and the federal one for that matter— will never get too hot for "massa" to bear.

A Long-Memoried Woman[1]

IN NOVEMBER, 1985, AN AMNESIAC turned up in Italy; he believed himself Canadian, and evidence for his belief, the *Toronto Star* reported, lay in what he remembered— three names: Joe Clark, Brian Mulroney and Pierre Trudeau. Three men; three whites; three politicians. I remember laughing— not at the amnesiac— but at the detritus of his memory and at the savage workings of the unconscious. What if David (he believed this was his name), the amnesiac, had remembered three women— *any* three women would do— Jeanne Sauvé, Flora McDonald or dear Mila. Or what if he had remembered Louis Riel, or Mary Ann Shadd, the first African Canadian journalist in Ontario, or even the word Haida, or Grassy Narrows? Had I read too much into what this man remembered; and should any more significance be attached to the residue of memory, other than the possibility that he may have, shortly prior to losing his memory, read a newspaper article mentioning these three men?

I chose to see significance in what David remembered: it identified him and put him in context. I chose also to draw an analogy between the loss of his memory, what was left, and the attempted erasure of the memories of the Africans brought as slaves to the New World. In the latter case, what was left would also be of significance.

The policy of all slave-holding nations was to wipe clean the mind of the African slave; how else prevent rebellion, ensure passive workers and guarantee good Christians? The effect of this policy was the separation, wherever possible, of African slaves from others of the same linguistic groups. Slave-owners prohibited and punished the expression of African culture, language, music, religion, or dress, thereby denying any validity to the African world view. Whatever remained of this process must, I believe, be inestimably precious and significant; as in the case of the amnesiac, it identifies and places in context the descendants of those first Africans in the New World. "They had," Katharine Dunham says of them, "an inborn intelligence to know if they kept up their tribal movements and rituals they would be saving themselves."[2]

In the course of writing a long poem recently, I listed some of the reasons why I consciously try to remember what did not happen to me personally, but which accounts for my being here today: to defy a culture that wishes to forget; to rewrite a history that at best forgot and omitted, at worst lied; to seek psychic reparations; to honour those who went before; to grieve for that which was irrevocably lost (language, religion, culture), and those for whom no one grieved; to avoid having to start over again (as so many oppressed groups have had to do); to "save ourselves." In making the list (by no means exhaustive) I found that even the mere determination to remember can, at times, be a revolutionary act— like the slave who refused to forget his or her rituals, or music, or whose body refused to forget the dance. All these acts of remembrance are, I believe, in the service of saving ourselves; as well, they replenish the scanty fund of memory we Africans in the West were left with, but which identified us, as indisputably as David's memory did.

Too many on both sides of the journey and the problem have forgotten the fifteen million that perished in the Middle Passage; too many are even more eager to forget the millions who continue to live marginalized lives because of that journey. (There is the Cosby show after all.) Far too many exhibit the social amnesia which, as Russell Jacoby argues in his work by the same name, results when the "vital relationship between mind and memory turns malignant; oblivion and novelty feed off each other and flourish."[3]

Some events, however, help to stimulate the memory: the revolution taking place within South Africa being just such an event. I can but only imagine the life of the black South African in Soweto or Cross Roads, but I remember; I remember what I do not know and have never lived, whenever I read of the death of yet another Black in South Africa; and when I witness the obscene contortions of the white Western powers over the imposition of sanctions, and their fundamental refusal to act in any meaningful way, I remember; I remember that the slave trade only came to an end when it was no longer economically feasible for the slave-owning, slave-trading nations; I remember the Wilberforces and the many others who, like those who condemn South Africa today, saw the appalling immorality of the trade in Black humans, and I remember that their platforms only gained credence when those nations— France, England, Spain, the United States— many of the same ones who today refuse to impose sanctions, saw that the continuance of the trade meant economic suicide.

I remember. And I believe that only when apartheid becomes too expensive for the West, will the latter become unequivocal in its condemnation and willingness to act. I remember, and believe that most Africans of the New and Old Worlds— even

those who think they have left the struggle a long way behind—
remember. In remembering, I hope they see the continuum that
stretches from the West across the Atlantic, across the centuries
to South Africa, and those early Africans who came west—
unwillingly. It is probably the greatest honour we pay the
millions that died on that journey, as well as those who died on
land— to remember.

Deep in my soul I remember; je me souviens; "I'se a
long-memoried woman."[1]

END NOTES:

1. Article title and final quote from a poem by English Caribbean poet Grace
Nichols.
2. From the film *Divine Drumbeat,* in which Katherine Dunham, African
American anthropologist and dancer, records her involvement with and study
of Haitian dance and religion.
3. Russell Jacoby, *Social Amnesia.*

Journal Entries Against Reaction

Damned If We Do and Damned If We Don't

(1) How does the writing of Black women mesh with Canadian feminist culture?

(2) Is it to be analyzed as a part of feminist culture or as Other?

(3) Is the writing of Black women to be included in this anthology because it is now the correct position to do so?

(4) How many of the articles on architecture, theatre, literature, the visual arts, video, and film explore how these art forms impinge on Black women, women of colour, or Native women, or even white working class women?

(5) How many of these articles will explore the absence of these women and their realities from the practice of these art forms?

THESE WERE THE QUESTIONS I raised in a letter in response to being asked to write an article on "Black women's writing" for the anthology *Works in Progress* (Rhea Tregebov, editor, The Women's Press).

I answered the questions myself:

(1) It doesn't. Canadian feminist culture is predominantly white— Anglo or Francophone. The writings of, and by, Black women are, for the most part, perceived as immigrant, exotic, or ethnographic, all of which translate into exclusion or marginalization.
(2) As Other— for the reasons given in (1) above.
(3) Yes.
(4) I don't know.
(5) I don't know.

My letter continued:

... my observation of feminism as articulated in the media and arts reveals a very specific type of feminism, which is continually articulated in an all-embracing fashion with the appropriate adjective— Black, working-class— appended when necessary. What remains unacknowledged is that a very culturally specific sense of female identity is being manipulated— and one that is acutely ahistorical in its failure to acknowledge race and class as anything more than economic and social categories.

In an honest response to my concerns, I was told that "as white women organizing an anthology of this sort, we're in a damned if we do and damned if we don't position." This aphorism also sums up the dilemma Black women continually face, though for very different reasons: they are, after all, seldom in the position of having to question their own power. Their damnation, on the contrary, arises too often from having too little choice. If the organizers were feeling damned at times— albeit for very different reasons— it was not a bad thing, I thought: it might help them to understand the no-win situations that often circumscribe the lives of Black women.

My other response to this explanation was the thought that if some of the issues I canvassed in my opening paragraph and my letter had been analyzed prior to the call for submissions, then this feeling of frustration and helplessness— this sense of trying to do the right thing, but not getting credit for it, which is undoubtedly the origin of the damned-if-we-do-and-damned-if-we-don't dilemma, could have been avoided. I have since come to believe otherwise. The aphorism *does* accurately sum up the position of those who have traditionally wielded power and are now trying to do something about it.

"Damned if we do and damned if we don't." Can't we just hear the well-intentioned male uttering these words as he struggles with his sexism and offends everyone? And he *is* damned— whether he does or doesn't. By history, by his gender, by his class at this time— by circumstances, in fact, which he himself may have had nothing to do with. And merely by virtue of belonging to a particular group, or class, or gender at a particular point in history, he shares in a certain collective responsibility, or guilt— a word I am very leery of using. If, however, we understand the historical underpinnings of his position, we must also acknowledge his frustration at not being accepted and at being challenged when he is being his most feminist. Damned he is.

While I, personally, have done nothing to increase the misery and suffering of those who live in developing countries, by virtue of living in the West, and partaking, however unwillingly, in some of the advantages that come from living here I, too, am implicated and share in the responsibility the West must take for the plight of many of these countries. My morning cup of cappuccino is closely linked to the skewing of these cash-crop economies to the consumption habits of the West.

The organizers of this anthology may have felt, justifiably, that they were acting correctly in trying to include Black women— and they were; but because of their historical position as white women at this particular point in time, and because of what this has meant and continues to mean in terms of power and exploitation, they *are* damned— if they do and if they don't. They have, in fact, joined the club of those whose choices have often, if not always, been the lesser of two evils. They are probably being damned for the sins of their forefathers and foremothers and, undoubtedly, some of their own.

However unfortunate it may be, we do live in times when a number of old scores are being settled, and a white skin is often considered evidence enough that somewhere there *are* scores to settle. To cast it in less biblical and Old Testament terms, these are times when people's expectations concerning their human and civil rights run high— often outstripping the ability of society to fulfil them— and old oppressions run deep and rankle.

The white feminist has, in certain situations, also been the beneficiary, at the expense of Black women and women of colour, of the spoils of patriarchy. She has been oppressed and exploited because of her gender, but she has also benefitted because of her skin, and continues to do so up to the present time. Consider, for example, that most affirmative action programs instituted by the various levels of government have now become synonymous with affirmative action *for women*— read white women, not peoples of other colours, nor the physically challenged.

No amount of good intentions, however well placed, will efface these historical and political realities; to pretend otherwise is to attempt to erase history. It is this evacuation of the historical and the political that informs the "feminism" we read about; this attempt to present feminism in Canada as something other than what it is— a predominantly white, middle class movement— is what I challenged in my letter to the organizers.

Once again, however, I had found myself in a reactive position— I was putting out energy and joining issue over what is essentially a non-issue for me— white feminism. Before I could even get to the issue of the writings by Black women (vis-à-vis Black women's writing), I had to engage in a question of self-definition.

For instance, if the organizers of the anthology have established such a category as Black women's writing, doesn't this imply that the other writings ought to be identified as white women's writing? Black women's writing can only exist as a category if white women's writing exists as a similar category. And who is defining whom? It was these questions which drove me back to an article I had written some months ago, but which addressed the core issue here for me— the issue of reaction and being reactive.

In "Why the United States," Julia Kristeva writes,

[As] everyone knows every negation is a definition. An "opposing" position is therefore determined by what is being opposed. And in this way we arrive at two antithetical systems which internalize and reflect one another's qualities...[1]

Is not the category Black women's writing an opposing position to white women's writing and, therefore, determined by it? And don't these two categories then internalize and reflect the other's qualities, the one being what the other is not and vice versa?

Neither explanation nor instruction is my purpose, and

continual self-definition "in opposition to" is an exhausting business. To deny while at the same time affirming is often an impossible task, and so as a writer who considers herself doubly blessed in being female and Black, my chief concern has been to create a place where I can write from a position of statement— first statement— and not reaction, because reaction implies that I am being determined by what I oppose.

No writer ever truly makes a first statement: we are all engaged in some form of dialogue with history, with literature, with the past, the present— even the future— expanding, clarifying, or modifying what someone else has already said, or trying to say it in some new way. "First statement" implies not so much the original or new statement, as a perspective from which I seek to write; a perspective that tries to embrace the full range of human experience in my work: struggle as well as love, politics *and* pleasure, sensuality, passion, sexuality, hatred— the grime and gold of the human spirit. As I write these words, I recall Toni Morrison's *The Song of Solomon*, a work that for me encompasses this profundity of human experience.

It is difficult, if not impossible, for Black female writers in the West today to ignore issues of racism or sexism in their works, particularly in realistic works, without making them seem untrue to life. The problem is not that we, Black and female writers, should be seeking to avoid these issues, but how to manage them within our work so that when we are done, the work is not consigned to the ghettos reserved for us (even in literature), where we become mouthpieces for the guilty, white, liberal conscience.

The challenge today for Black women writers is to subvert those restrictions that subtly, and not so subtly, suggest we should only write about certain topics, in certain ways; we will have to find new ways of including our wholeness in our work while maintaining our integrity as Black women. In my own work I have witnessed a poem move from the raw, brutal emotion arising out of the absence of a mother tongue, to a poem that now contains and sustains that grief and moves beyond it, even to celebration.

Surrealist forms, the magic realism of Latin American writers (which those of us from the Caribbean can lay claim to), post-modernist eruptions into the text of other discourses, all offer the possibility of embracing the unembraceable— our struggles *and* our passions. Whatever method we choose to elaborate our realities, the imperative is a discovery and recon-struction of ourselves piece by piece, in our own images. This, perhaps, is the best way the Black female writer has at her disposal to expose the lie that has constructed her as Other, *without engaging in reaction.*

"Journal Entries Against Reaction," which follows, speaks to this issue— a central issue in my life as a writer circumscribed by the two political realities of being female and Black. It is not a piece *about* Black women's writing since that would be a reaction to white women's writing. What it attempts to do in this context is to convert negation into affirmation. It prescribes no answers, but merely charts the terrain and raises issues. It is one writer's statement— a writer who often feels equally damned— if she does and if she doesn't; a writer who is continually assaulted by the tenets of sexism and white supremacy, and who, for that reason, struggles to resist the temptation to reaction in her writing.

JOURNAL ENTRIES AGAINST REACTION

DAY ONE

We bleed, therefore we are. In opposition to the *cogito ergo sum* of Cartesian philosophy, which would have us believe something as simple and reflexive as thinking proves our existence. Surely only a man— a white male at that— could have made such a suggestion. Images which confront me daily in the media suggest that for the Others— Blacks, people of colour, the Native peoples, women, gays— my aphorism is a more accurate one: we bleed, therefore we are. We have, after all, been thinking ever since we *were*; much of the time it appears that we still are *not*. I take liberties with Descartes' maxim, but for me it is not only rooted in his philosophical ideas on the certainty of doubt, but also in a patriarchal matrix. I think, therefore I am. Only a man.

DAY TWO

"[T]he first impulse of the Black man [sic] is to say no to those who attempt to build a definition of him. It is understandable that the first action of the Black man is a reaction..."[2] Much the same may be said of women— their first action a reaction to those who "build definitions" of them. It is difficult not to react— as female, as Black— when much around conspires against these very realities. And why shouldn't one react?

DAY THREE

There is nothing wrong in reacting. We must. But there are dangers for the writer who has roots in these twin realities—

Blackness and femaleness. The danger is that one's writing can easily become persistently— I am tempted to say perniciously— reactive. Can writing which is always reactive ever succeed beyond the immediate and particular? Can it ever be more than a rallying cry to action? Should it be more? or less? or different? Rallying cries are absolutely imperative. But if we consistently write from a reactive position, are we not still responding to someone else's agenda?

DAY FOUR

Racism, sexism and all the other 'isms call forth and inspire reaction. To write from a place of wholeness and integrity— is such an ideal utopian in today's world— writing as a Black female?

DAY FIVE

The white male thinks, and therefore is. He seldom, if ever, says or needs to say, I am; I am white; I am male; I am human. Everything around him conspires to transform mere attributes into qualities of apparent permanence and universality, synonymous with privilege. We might say these arguments are hackneyed and old hat— we are, after all, in the age of post-feminism. But these issues crash in against the writing which is rooted in the word— "the 'paternal Word' sustained by a fight to the death between the two races (men/women)."[3] Not to mention the father tongues imposed on us, the colonized peoples of colour. How to use the "paternal Word" to issue forth first statements— of wholeness?

DAY SIX

The Black, female writer faces a dilemma. Integral to the qualities of white maleness is a denial— at times more explicit than at others— of all that she is and represents. She must respond and react. The conundrum: how to transform what is essentially a response and a reaction into its own first statement.

DAY SEVEN

To transform writing from reaction to statement. To oppose Woman to Man, according to Kristeva, is to impose a "fixed sexual identity which is counterproductive to understanding and action."[4] Woman is not a reaction to Man; she is not a response. She is her own first statement. Black is not a reaction to white; it is its own first statement. I am only Black and female, if you are white and male. I think, therefore I am. Black and female.

DAY EIGHT

How to convert the mere attributes of Blackness and female-ness into first principles, as gratuitous as whiteness and male-ness? Or are feminism and Black consciousness but moments— spasms in the history of *man*kind?

DAY NINE

I am. Not in defiance and response to your pretending otherwise. But simply because I am. Not because I bleed— unless you bleed with me. But because I think. I demand the utter luxury and privilege of claiming existence merely by virtue of my thoughts— they have not been sufficient to date— not even my blood. Is it possible— to think and so be? Probably not in our time. But as I write, I am constantly establishing myself, my being, my reality. As centre, not Other. To echo Kristeva's question about women— what will they write that is new? What will I write that is new?

DAY TEN

A Caucasianist (as in Africanist): a specialist (not by choice) in Caucasian affairs. I once introduced myself at a poetry reading in this way— a Caucasianist. A stab at the constant imposition of the white Western expert on the rest of the world's peoples. We who have lived in the belly of the whale— shark is maybe more accurate a symbol— for so long, surely, we know best its internal workings and their outward manifestations; surely we— "the Others"— are the true experts. One seemingly absurd attempt at positioning myself at centre, not periphery. There are more serious attempts: developing a language more attuned to expressing my reality; creating written forms of the demotic languages of the Caribbean— in which I am most at home— as in Heidegger's sense of language being the house of being; "playing with" language to arrive at that place where life and death meet within the language. Language itself— symbol of death and life for me. To arrive at the centre. To write from the centre.

DAY ELEVEN

There is no law against dreaming. So writes Winnie Mandela. Dreaming— the imagination— the one faculty of the human that can resist colonization. To construct imaginative and poetic worlds *as if* we were at the centre. To design imaginative and poetic scapes with us at the centre. We speak from the centre and are whole.

DAY TWELVE

How to transform reaction into statement. Transformation or metamorphosis— "the action or process of changing in form or substance, esp. by magic or witchcraft." (OED) All art is about transformation and metamorphosis, which requires sacrifice: one form or shape, one reality given up or sacrificed for another. All art is about sacrifice— of one sort or another: the artist lets go, literally gives up on the faith that something else will appear. Magic? Witchcraft? It often does appear to be. To transform reaction into statement, what must be sacrificed?

DAY THIRTEEN

Call and response. An African art form. Together the call and the response make up the whole expression, or the expression of the whole. Denial and response. They can never coexist together: they can never coexist because denial implies death of the Other, and there is no response to death. Denial and response— mutually exclusive.

DAY FOURTEEN

We are, however, more than the sum of all of our parts. To believe that our reality is circumscribed by the words Black or female is to connive and collude in our own prisons. But. But. But.

DAY FIFTEEN

Writing cannot be in defense but in acceptance— of life, of death— it must transcend— but how to find the centre from which one can look out— all around— transcending gender, race, class, yet still belonging to all those things— because we are, after all, human *and* flawed.

DAY SIXTEEN

And on the sixteenth day she looked at her work created in her i-mage and she was well pleased.

The second portion of this article is based on an article published in FUSE, Winter 86/87, No. 43.

END NOTES:

1. Julia Kristeva, *The Kristeva Reader*, Toril Moi, editor, Oxford: Basil Blackwell, 1986, p. 274.
2. Franz Fanon, *Black Skin, White Masks*, New York: Grove Press, 1967, p. 36.
3. Kristeva, op. cit.
4. Ibid.

Women and Theft

SEVERAL MONTHS AGO I WAS ASKED to take part in a panel discussion at the Arts Against Apartheid Festival— the theme: "Women and Poverty." I don't know what it must be like to be truly poor— having no options as well as having no money (I can only imagine it). Since I stopped practising law at a legal clinic many years ago, my contact with poor people has been limited. So what could I say about women and poverty that would be new and not a repetition of old and hackneyed platitudes? What bothered me about the theme— "women and poverty"— was how well the words went together— as if they belonged together— women and poverty— like motherhood and apple pie.

I went to Rabbi Klein's *Dictionary of Etymology* for help. *Poverty*, he told me, came from the word *pauper*, meaning *poor*. Next I checked with Oxford, and they— all men undoubtedly— told me that poor was the state of having few or no material possessions— *that*, I could identify with; the opposite of rich— we were getting a little closer to the meat of the issue here. I went back to the Rabbi, and he told me that *poor* was also the descendant of *pauper*, which in turn was a combination of two words meaning *one who produces little*. One who produces little. Women? Women produce little. Women are poor because they produce little. None of that made any sense as I thought of the vast quantities of work women have traditionally done. They are presently responsible for two thirds of all working hours in the world.

I went back to Rabbi Klein on the subject of being rich; he told me that the origin of *rich* was to be found in being kingly— not queenly, but kingly.

Kings, paupers, and women— I was on to something here, I felt. I certainly wouldn't have said that kings were noted for producing much— if they have had a great deal of material wealth and displayed it, this has usually been as a result of others producing— much or little— and being forced to give it up to the king, or having it taken away to make kings rich. And if the opposite of rich is poor— the state of producing little— surely we're entitled to assume that one of the qualities of being rich is producing much. Surely. But logic is not something the English language is noted for, and here were those kings— who hadn't produced much— in close association with the word *rich*, of which *poor* was the opposite. But I now had much more than I started out with— women, kings, and between them, poverty— the condition of being poor or producing little.

If we accept that women have traditionally produced much— and the statistics exist to support this— how do we get from the state of producing much and having little, to being described as producing little? Was there a word that could describe the process by which kings who produced little were made rich, and women who produced much became poor? I came at it another way— if women produced much and now had little, it was either because they gave it away, lost it, or had it taken away from them. I knew they hadn't lost it; in some instances they may have given it away out of love for their families, but since they were very seldom, if ever, free agents, you couldn't really call it giving; so that left the last explanation.

Theft. "Women and Theft" became the subject of my presentation. The word poverty, I argued, really only described the end result, omitting the process, the pattern and series of actions which, over the centuries, has resulted in the inevitable link between women and poverty.

I was, as I often do, playing with words in a very serious way in the hope of their releasing some hidden or forgotten meaning. What I hadn't known at the time was that there was very good reason, with a long and distinguished pedigree, why the words *women* and *poverty* belonged together. It lay in the distinction, traditionally unacknowledged, as Hannah Arendt argues, between labour and work.

This distinction, according to Arendt, has been largely ignored in political thought and modern labour theories, yet it is reflected in all European languages, in the existence of different words for these two activities— *labour* and *work*— although these words are used interchangeably and almost synonymously.

Traditionally, *work* has referred to that activity which produces new objects— objects that added to the world of things, and often outlasted the humans that made them. *To labour* meant to do work whose products or results were consumed immediately; objects, if produced, were produced only incidentally. The distinguishing mark of labour lay in the immediate consumption of its products; its significance in its essentiality: without labour life was not liveable. Under the general rubric of labour we can include cooking, cleaning and general caretaking, all of which are indispensable to living. Despite its essential quality, however, or probably *because* of it, every attempt was made to keep this type of work and those who did it— women and slaves— hidden and away from public life. "Women were hidden away," writes Arendt, "not only because they were somebody else's property, but because their life was laborious, devoted to bodily functions." A classic case of blaming the victim.

Labour or non-productive work didn't enrich the world, reasoned those early thinkers; it resulted in nothing because its results were consumed immediately, leaving nothing behind— except, of course, more labour. These men were appropriately contemptuous of this type of work and those carrying it out. They were wrong, of course. Labour did produce something of value— of inestimable value: the freedom and potential productivity of masters and men; freedom to pursue whatever public activity they were engaged upon. It would take Marx to recognize the surplus value in the labouring activity itself, and to articulate how the labour of some would suffice for the life of all. But in the history of Western thought— reflected in the language— labour and poverty belonged together, since "the activity corresponding to the status of poverty was labouring."

All of which takes us right back to kings— the rich— and paupers who produce little. The contradiction at the heart of the word *poor* is patent, if we follow Arendt's argument, for poor people have not only produced much, or laboured much, but they have had much taken away from them, and were then described as producing little. The word itself now encapsulates, reflects, perpetuates and so magnifies the theft. And within the traditional category of the poor were women, whose work was laborious. So the words *women* and *poverty* did belong together after all. Historically. Socially. Politically. Etymologically.

So what? We know about the oppression of women— by men, by the patriarchy— and am I not just stating the obvious? Perhaps, but the obvious is still not yet received opinion, and the statistics that appear in Robin Morgan's *Sisterhood Is Global* help buttress my argument that what we ought to be talking about is women and theft: "women represent one half the global population, one third of the labour force, yet they receive only one tenth of the world income and own less than one tenth of world property."

But there is more to it than that. What I'm interested in is how language continues to betray itself, its sources and its context— how it continues to imprison us. My question is this: is there anything to be gained by talking of women and theft, rather than women and poverty? I believe so. Poverty describes a state— a rather passive state, and most public discussion on the issue of poverty pays little attention to how the state of poverty is brought about— how integrally related it is to our own system.

As a Black woman, when I think of women and theft, I make the immediate association with even more blatant forms of theft that Black women— and men— in the New World were subject to— not only theft of their labour, but of their spouses, their children, their religion, their culture and their languages. So too the Native peoples of the New World. In the universally tragic contact of the West with other cultures, the leitmotif of theft and impoverishment will always be found.

Maybe it's my arrant belief in the power of the word, but it seems to me that if we start talking about women— Black and non-Black women— and theft, we have to start asking questions like who did the stealing (and in some cases women stole from women as well), and what was stolen. In some instances theft of material possessions, or of remuneration for one's labour, was the least of the crimes committed. Maybe we can even start talking about reparations for women, instead of affirmative action. What are we affirming? That women have been victims of theft for centuries, or men's overwhelming generosity in recognizing themselves as thieves? Strong language? Perhaps. But what I am most interested in revealing is that even when we believe we are being objectively descriptive by using a word like poverty, or poor, we continue the myth that poor people are poor because they are poor— they produce little; we have all, I'm sure, heard the modern variation of that argument about Blacks, Native people, and women.

So let's really start reconstructing the language that surrounds us— here's a start: instead of aid to Africa, let's start talking about reparations to Africa (the first word suggests hand-outs, the latter acknowledges the existence of a wrong); instead of women and poverty, let's talk about women and theft— then let's talk some more about compensation for that theft.

A tall order? Undoubtedly. But as a writer nurtured on the bile of a colonial language, whose only intent was imperialistic, I see no way around the language, only through it, challenging the mystification and half truths at its core.

The Sick Butterfly

South Africa's War Against Children

Life nowadays is like a sick butterfly. To many of us it is not worth living when it is like this...The little kids don't understand why they have been put in jail.— Bothale (age 12)

When I am old I would like to have a wife and to children a boy and a girl and a big house and to dogs and freedom.
— Moagi (age 8)

TWO DOGS AND FREEDOM– *Children of the Township Speak Out* is the title of the book from which these two excerpts come. The book arose out of an English lesson during the 1985 South African emergency, and the children whose thoughts and feelings about the emergency appear in the book are between the ages of eight and 15. They attend Open School, an extra-mural cultural and educational project in Johannesburg, and it was the intensity of the children's feelings and thoughts that persuaded the school to publish their work.

Originally banned on the grounds that it contained "twisted and dangerous images of happenings in South Africa," the book was considered a threat against the state because it was "aimed at an adult market. It hopes to evoke empathy for township school children. It portrays them as suffering because of mass oppression... The book undermines *white confidence in the morality of the law*"[1] [my emphasis]. On appeal the ban was lifted.

Black children in South Africa have always suffered the effects of the war against their parents— poor nutrition, inadequate housing, substandard schooling and economic exploitation. The last few years, however, have seen a new development— the brutal attack by the state against children and young people. In 1982, eight children under 18 were detained by the state; in 1984, nine; in 1986, more than 2,000 under 16 were detained, and these only in the emergency areas. According to statistics collected by the Detainees' Parents Support Committee (DPSC), in the five months after the June 12, 1986 emergency, some 22,000 people were detained and 40% of those were under 18 years of age. Eight-thousand-eight-hundred children at the rate of 250 per week had been detained in this period— some as young as eight or nine years of age and, in at least one documented case, a baby four months old.

How does a state wage war against children, and why? Is it that South Africa perceives children as a real threat to its security, and are we, therefore, to conclude that the armed might of the South African state is truly threatened by children as young as eight or nine years of age? What does this tell us, if we need to know more, about such a state? And further to the issue— how do children lay aside what we have come to think of as childhood, to come to the flash point of taking on a state upon whose brutality they have been weaned? Is this an aberration of childhood, or more accurate a manifestation of the potential of children, than the rampant consumerism and political sloth displayed by Western youth? Or is it merely reflective of the urgency of the situation in South Africa?

These were some of the questions I asked myself as I tried to make sense of the figures and statistics quoted above— as I read the writings of the young authors of *Two Dogs and Freedom*.

What is childhood? Should children be protected from war at all costs, or should they be allowed to take the course of their lives into their own hands as Black South African children have done? It had not been the first time these thoughts had occurred to me. I entertained them when, in 1976, I read of the June 16 massacre in Soweto that indiscriminately and wantonly killed school children who were only claiming what was theirs by birth— their land, and by right— the determination of their own and their children's future. In "The News at Nine," a poem I wrote at the time, I described "a child meeting bullets with books/...striking a deathly bargain/blood for being/..." I entertained these thoughts again during the crisis of Maurice Bishop's government in Grenada; there school children marched to the airport in an attempt to close it. I wrote then, in a still unnamed poem, of "the children who take to the street/following a pied piper intent on revenge/the child who cannot spell/the act of commitment or courage it intends/a small body outgrown by the idea...who says childhood was not meant for this?"

Once again I entertain these thoughts as I read of this war against children and how cheaply Black life is held, not only there but throughout the world. I consider my own Black children and wonder how much state power it would take to blow them away, lose them or destroy their minds.

As a parent, I am both profoundly disturbed and drawn to the phenomenon of children at war, or involved in war, either as victims or on behalf of the state which, to my mind, is another form of victimization. Protection, guidance and education— love:

war undermines and subverts all these parental functions; it undermines the overall confidence of those who produce life and wish to nurture it to fruition.

Here in the West, where we have, to date, been fortunate or cunning enough to avoid war and armed struggle, childhood is a luxury. The most challenging event white parents face is the extended "agony" of adolescence and all that that encompasses (and it *can* be a severely destructive period for both parent and child). There is also the spectre of youth unemployment. Black parents have the added problems of police harassment and pernicious racism that undermine their children's sense of worth. Comparison is odious, but laid alongside the challenges facing their Black counterparts in South Africa, Western children and young people are comfortably off.

My comparison, however, is not merely for the sake of comparison, and to say that South African children are worse off than their Western counterparts advances nothing. What it does do for me, however, is heighten the two extreme examples of what childhood might be all about, and much as I abhor the society which seduces its young people with false claims of advertisement, and suggests no greater aim for them than making money, having a good life-style and drinking the right kind of beer, I am as disturbed by a society that forces its children to abandon childhood and enter the arena of war.

Childhood as we know it in the West is a relatively recent phenomenon. In Greek literature, children were used primarily as props, as they were too in the Judeo-Christian tradition, although the latter presumed the existence of a soul, even within the littlest child. Jesus may have suffered "little children to come unto him," but up to the fifteenth century, with the exception of the Madonna and child, children do not appear in Western literature. Until relatively recently, protection of the child for itself was not a clearly recognized value in the West, and for the most part children were considered miniature adults, with even their clothing being replicas of adult clothing. Consider also the Fifth Crusade in 1212 known as the Children's Crusade: thousands of young people from France and Germany set out to free the Holy Land from the infidel, only to be lost, ship-wrecked or sold into slavery.

With the coming of the Industrial Revolution in the eigh-teenth century, working class child labour became a way of life, while the fortunes made by the middle and upper classes guaranteed their children the cossetting and protection denied others. It is only as we get into the twentieth century that society begins to accept that *all* children require protection from eco-nomic exploitation, and to recognize that childhood is an experience of significance and to be valued. During this period we see the development of psychoanalytic theory validating the child as parent of the adult; legislation "protecting" the child and establishing compulsory education for children also begins to enter the statute books of most Western countries. Compare this history of childhood in the West, albeit abbreviated, with what Graham Greene observed in the nineteen-thirties as he travelled through Western Liberia:

Love, it has been said, was invented in Europe by the troubadours, but it existed here without the trappings of civilization. They were tender towards their children (I seldom heard a crying child, unless at the sight of a white face, and never saw one beaten).[2]

Belfast, Cambodia, Viet Nam, Iran, Palestine, Lebanon— by no means an exhaustive list, but these are some of the countries that come to mind when the issue of children at war arises. In Belfast, children were and are, I presume, still involved in partisan strife, more as extensions of their parents' struggles. When these children became the focus of media attention, their involvement was presented within the context of them growing up surrounded by tension, hostilities and strife as an everyday aspect of life.

In Cambodia, the Khmer Rouge drafted children into their death squads which were directed against all intellectuals and, as often as not, against other children. In his book, *Children of War*,[3] Roger Rosenblatt describes a young Cambodian girl in a refugee camp drawing pictures of a portable guillotine she was forced to use against other children who refused to work. The bizarre aspect of this mutilating war was that the Khmer Rouge believed it was purging the country of corruption and preparing children for a better life.

As in all war zones, Vietnamese children suffered the terrorism, guerilla raids and bombings that were a part of that war. There was, however, no evidence that children were used or singled out as a group in any particular way.

In Lebanon, children, women and old people comprise the majority in the Palestinian refugee camps; bombing raids against these camps, such as those against Shatila and Sabra must, therefore, be seen as directed against those groups. The public reason given by Israel for these raids was that the camps harboured terrorists; whether or not we accept this reason, what is significant here is that there is no stated policy of singling out women or children as targets of war. Some may argue that it is irrelevant what the stated policy is, if the result is the same— the killing of children.

In Iran, the state encouraged young boys— some as young

as 13 or 14— to volunteer to fight against Iraq. In the West, the drafting of young teen-aged children into the army would be considered an abuse of childhood; in Iran, however, both children and parents believed they were doing their duty to Allah.

The situation in South Africa differs from all of the above examples. There the full force of the state is brought to bear, in a protracted period of attack, against virtually all Black children in the townships, and no place is sacrosanct— least of all the home or the school.

What has distinguished South African children has been the role they have come to play, as students, in South African politics. It is this involvement in politics, in an organized way, that presents another picture of childhood than the one we have grown accustomed to. The DPSC report cites, among others, the following reasons for their involvement: greater energy; more effective state control of parents and adults than youth; less relevant police measures for children; no familial responsibilities; idealism and courage.

Children often show a readiness to endure everything for their beliefs, especially when their detention memories are no longer debilitary to them. The small luxuries of life, although they are enjoyed tremendously when available, do not consume their attention. Children are prepared to deny all sorts of privileges and comforts for "the struggle." They will work tirelessly at organizing their communities and see it as a great honour to simply be involved in working for a better future for all.

The Bantu Education Act has become the focus of much of the organization by students. This act prescribes that the African should be educated to "meet the demands which the economic life of South Africa will impose upon him." The cornerstone of these educational policies was the precept that the African had to be taught from childhood: that "equality with the Europeans [was] not for them." Their advocacy and organization as students against the educational policies, as contained in this act, singled them out as targets in June, 1976, and again in 1985, 1986, and 1987. The impact of student organization has been such that "the adults who felt rejected by them 10 years ago, look to them now for direction in many communal matters, and increasingly consult them over decisions to be taken."

The campaign of state terror against children has been indiscriminate, with "non-involved," non-activist children being as vulnerable to arrest and detention as activists and organizers. The list of abuses by the state against Black children is long; it details how the "protector" of children, the state— South Africa does have child protection legislation— has become the abuser of children. Random detention of children; their torture in detention including threats of necklacing; the bombing of their homes; failure to inform families, legal guardians or lawyers of their arrest and detention; unsanitary, overcrowded conditions in detention; inadequate medical attention in detention (there have been reports of children cutting out bullets themselves rather than going to seek medical aid); lack of adequate food in detention; very little or no exercise; incarceration with adults, sometimes criminals; random shooting (against children) by the armed forces, as well as vigilantes, at funeral vigils, or on their way to and from school or shops.

These examples are but a sample of the documented activities by the South African government in its war against its children. Parents are often so confused and distressed at the disappearance of their children and their inability to find them, that many express relief at finding them in the morgues. It puts an end to the endless, bureaucratic red tape that confounds their search, not to mention the expense of lawyers.

This regime that seeks to uphold "the morality of the law" has imprisoned an 11-year-old boy, Fanie Godika, for 57 days. While in prison Fanie, who was picked up while sheltering himself from the rain, was assaulted by police officers, black and white: "They kicked me with their big boots... they kicked me all over. They only stopped when my tooth came out."

In Soweto, an entire high school of some 1,200 students was arrested, herded into trucks and taken away. In the Northern Orange Free State, police and defense forces occupied a school and carried out beatings with the sjambok. "As soon as the siren sounds to end break, they immediately proceed to start whipping people into the classrooms. In another instance an entire family was arrested and held for a day— including two babies, four and seven months old respectively, as well as a three-year-old."

The DPSC report identifies three aims of this war against children: to obtain confessions, to obtain information on others, and general terrorism. To some degree the state does succeed, for the effect of its methods reverberates throughout the communities: children go on the run, fearing either imprisonment, or for the safety of their families and homes; families become even more fragmented; stress is increased on family members. Not least of all is the effect on the children themselves. Depression and anxiety are the two broad categories their symptoms cluster around. On the less negative side, the DPSC has noted that in some cases the incarceration of children has strengthened the family unit and wider community. One father's way of coping with the disappearance of his own children is to widen his parental responsibility:

There are so many of these children. We do not know where our
children are. Therefore we must help any child that we find and try
to give them some of the things that they can no longer get from
their parents. We must give them food, shelter, and love. Maybe in
another place it will be my child that is getting this, so I must give
to those I find. We all must.

This has been but an extremely abbreviated account of how
the South African government has set about to ravage further its
Black population. President Botha has recently decided to extend
the state of emergency, promising to fight the "terrorists" in
South Africa, and claiming his God-given moral authority to do
so. This from a man responsible for actions such as those
described above. Life is indeed a very sick butterfly when words
like morality are bandied about in this context. If ever South
Africa retained a scintilla of morality, it has now absolutely and
irrevocably abnegated it by waging war against its children. "It
becomes a crime against humanity when children are involved...
There is no justification for a war against children."[4] So testified
Eli Wiesel, Nobel peace laureate before the court trying Klaus
Barbie for the murder of 44 Jewish children. How astonishing
(and, perhaps, not so astonishing), therefore, the silence that has
greeted the persecution and incarceration of some 8,000 children
in South Africa.

Personal attachment, emotional stability and permanency of
educational influence were the three elements identified by Anna
Freud in her work, *War and Children*,[5] as essential in preventing
psychological malformations. With the possible exception of the
first, none of these needs are being met for Black South African
children, and undoubtedly South Africa will reap the harvest of
this brutal sowing for a long time to come. One thing we may

be certain of, is that state terrorism of the type described above will leave an indelible mark on the society as a whole.

I do not know if we have learnt any more about childhood from the experiences of Black South African children. These children who have taken on the brunt of hippos (a type of tank), tear gas, bullets and sjamboks, have done what they had to do; in so doing they have sacrificed a childhood to guarantee a future of some dignity and failing that, death. To attempt to maintain traditional distinctions in the face of Botha's regime is irrelevant, for the South African state has always warred against its Black children, albeit in more subtle ways, by depriving them of adequate nutrition, housing and schooling; by destroying their parents and their families; and more than anything else, by withholding their land.

What Black South African children have done, is brought that war from the shadows into the open— an act very much in keeping with what we know to be one of the gifts of childhood: the ability to articulate, often to the embarrassment of adults, exactly what it is they are experiencing, observing or feeling. All sorts of adages and aphorisms come to mind: "Out of the mouths of babes..." "A little child shall lead them..." By taking its war to the children, the South African regime has revealed just how morally bankrupt it is; it has also shown that it will go to any length to ensure the maintenance of the ideology of white supremacy.

In a country where the sick butterfly flutters and "little kids don't understand why they have been put in jail"— in such a country the children have become "sword and fire./Red ruin, and the breaking up of laws" (Tennyson). Despite my not being Christian, I find myself seeking biblical imagery to assist me in managing the evil that is South Africa. This imagery is, strangely, fitting given the claim of white South Africans to have founded the "kingdom of God" in South Africa. In a New Testament prediction which the disciple Matthew records, Jesus foretells that many strangers and foreigners will inherit "the promised land," but that "the children of the kingdom shall be cast out into outer darkness." Many strangers and foreigners have inherited South Africa, and its Black children have been "cast out into outer darkness," but to continue the prediction, South Africa is guaranteed great "weeping and gnashing of teeth."

END NOTES:

1. *Report of the Detainees' Parents Support Committee* (DPSC). Unless otherwise identified, all quotations are from this document.
2. *Journey Without Maps*, Graham Greene.
3. Garden City, New York: Anchor Press/Doubleday, 1983.
4. *Toronto Star*, June 3, 1987.
5. Anna Freud, *War and Children*, New York, Medical War Books, 1943.

How Do You Explain?

The Toronto Star:

How do you explain to an eight-year-old why, for the first time in the 20 years of living in Canada, his mother is afraid as a Black woman?

How do you explain that the year you came to this country was 1968, during one of the long hot summers in the United States, when dogs, hoses, mace and batons were used indiscriminately against Black people who dared to demand that they be treated with respect and dignity— as members of the human race, and that never having been in a predominantly white country, his mother was afraid? Were these white Canadians going to turn on her for being Black? They didn't, for this was Canada after all, and although she would come to understand that the history of racism was as deeply embedded in this country as in the U.S., overt racism appeared invisible.

How do you explain to an eight-year-old child that despite the fact that over those 20 years the myth of a non-racist Canada has been exploded time and again, as a place to raise young children in such a way that they grow up respecting themselves for what they are— African Canadians, respecting others and their differences, and most importantly taking pride in themselves and all their heritages, African, English, Caribbean and Canadian, Toronto was close to exceptional when compared with other large metropolitan areas in the U.S.?

How do you explain to a child that Black people do not want special treatment— they want to be treated as others are treated— that if 17 year old white boys are not shot for stealing cars, then 17 year old Black boys should not be shot. That's all. And how do you explain that when you get the feeling that the police consider you the enemy, merely for asking for that equality of treatment, it is very hard not to feel afraid?

It is very hard not to feel afraid and to teach your children not to be afraid when it appears that the police are angry with you as a group, because you demand what you ought not to have to demand— equality of treatment. It is very hard not to feel afraid when you read of threats by the police not to respond to incidents involving Black people— isn't this encouraging Blacks to be scapegoated, and in an already racist society, isn't this singling out an already vulnerable group and setting them up as potential targets for bigots?

How do you explain all this to a child, and the fact that as a group, Blacks have little or no power in this society, that there have been no major or massive demonstrations recently in response to the most recent shooting of a Black youth; that despite this Blacks have again been incorrectly accused of bringing pressure to bear to have a police officer charged. How do you explain that to want justice, as a Black person, in this society is to be described as an activist, which now appears to have the connotation of a four letter word?

And finally, how do you explain to a child how alone it is to be a Black person in Canadian society today— that there has not been much or any support from other groups in this society— where are the Jewish, Japanese, Chinese, or Indian Canadians; where the churches; where the political leaders in this face off between the Black community and one of the most powerful institutions in this city— the police force?

But explain I shall and explain I must— to myself and to my children small as they are, that racism is a scourge on any society and that *everyone* is victimized by it; explain I shall and explain I must, that we as African Canadians must and shall overcome.

Yours truly,
M. Nourbese Philip

Social Barbarism and the Spoils of Modernism

THE AUDITORIUM OF THE MCLAUGHLIN PLANETARIUM was spacious and bright; I was there to learn about African art: a four week series of lectures sponsored by the Royal Ontario Museum (ROM).[1] Around me the room was full of people, all white with the exception of five– including myself– Blacks. I didn't miss the overwhelming irony of my being there to find out about something I should have been as familiar with as I am with the beliefs and practices of Christianity– and I don't mean African "art" since that is a Western construct, but African culture. And I was not familiar with African culture– at least not in the sense of being intimate with it.

The reason for my presence in that room was, I felt, deeply rooted in the very events and circumstances that had brought the pieces, now on display, courtesy of the ROM, to the West and Canada: the same events that had brought the "primitive," the savage, the African– the Other– to the West in the form of "art" or aesthetics. The supreme irony in these events was that while the African aesthetic was being appropriated and manipulated to the West's own purposes; while African "art" was being extolled and praised– and at the same time being evacuated of any ritually appropriate meaning– the peoples of the continent from which these cultural objects originated were being oppressed, enslaved, and denied basic human rights.

It is pretty much received opinion now that the "art of tribal Africa was a major influence on Western art early this century and has remained so for decades."[2] For "major influence" I would substitute *indispensable debt*, for by the time the moderns came upon the idea of the "primitive," their artistic tradition had been depleted of much of its energy and vitality.

At the turn of the century European art had reached an impasse in its search for a new visual language sufficient to express the dynamics of the time. There was a growing discontent with the increased industrialization of European life. These two factors forced artists to look elsewhere for inspiration and spiritual solace— they turned to the ideas of primitivism and the exotic.[3]

This statement is, however, incomplete, for turning to the ideas of primitivism and the exotic would not have been possible for artists were it not for aggressive, expansionist, colonial policies of European powers. The two developments are inextricably linked— as linked as I was to those ROM pieces I had registered to learn about— and must be seen and understood together.

Erasure— levels and layers of erasure is what we get instead. Beginning with the artists themselves. Many of these artists— Picasso included— who drew their inspiration from the work of Africa and Oceania, were later to deny and rationalize the influence of this work on their own work. Picasso for instance denied ever having seen any "primitive" art until *after* he had painted "Les Demoiselles d'Avignon" in 1907. There is evidence, however, that Picasso had seen examples of African sculpture in the studios of Matisse and Derain in 1906, and by

1907 had begun to build his own collection.

Constantin Brancusi initially extolled the qualities of African sculpture; later, he was to disassociate himself from its influence, cautioning not only against imitating Africans, but also describing African sculpture as charged with "demonic forces." He even went so far as to destroy a number of his early pieces because, he claimed, they were too African.

Another of the moderns— Jacques Lipchitz— both collector and artist, denied that African art influenced his sculpture, but did concede— magnanimously— that "we shook hands with Negro art, but this is not an influence— merely an encounter." And what an encounter!— I am tempted to say of an indispensable kind. To these three we can add Epstein, Archpenko and others of the same period.

The trend to erasure still continues, for in 1984 the MOMA[4] exhibition on modern and primitive art went to great lengths to assign responsibility for cubism to the West: in the development of cubism as curated, tribal art would play a minor role, with the identification of affinities rather than *causal* influences.

Why this denial of the African? Writing early in this century on the subject of African sculpture, Roger Fry unwittingly provides some clue. In his opening paragraph of an essay entitled "Negro Art," he writes:

So deeply rooted in us is the notion that the Negro race is in some fundamental way not only inferior to others but almost subhuman, that it upsets our notion of fitness even to compare their creations with those of a people like the Greeks who we regard as almost super human.[5]

He goes further than any critic I have read in articulating the impact of African art on the West: "Modern art owes more to Negroes than to any other tradition... the contribution of Africa to the spiritual inheritance may turn out to be of the greatest importance." But the white supremacist approach he identifies in the opening paragraph explains much of the erasure.

"Primitive"— "primitivism." I have, so far, thrown these words around without defining them, not at all because I assume there is shared agreement on their meanings. These are words I am uncomfortable with, carrying as they do so much of the connotative imperialist baggage of the West. The dictionary meaning of *primitive* merely asserts the concept of being first, or early, which is at the etymological heart of the word. Today's connotations imply the savage, the illogical, the irrational, the dark side— all the West wished to project outwards on to others.

My sense is that if the primitive did not exist— as in the early peoples with non-industrialized, non-capitalist modes of production, the West would still have found it necessary to invent the concept of primitivism. There is a quantum leap from the early peoples and their cultures to the concept of primitivism, the underpinnings of which is colonialism. As Hal Foster argues in his essay "The 'Primitive' Unconscious,"[6] primitivism became a device to manage the primitive which the West would have found too disruptive or transgressive.

What the West sought and got from Africa and Oceania was necessary, not only from the perspective of art and aesthetics, but also from the perspective of the psyche. Identify, describe, catalogue, annotate, appropriate— these words best sum up the West's relationship with Africa— the Other, against which are arrayed the forces of reason, rationality, logic and knowledge as possessable and certifiable. European powers would rationalize economic exploration of these areas by theories of racial and cultural superiority, equating the Other with all that was inferior.

With the "approach" of the West to these early cultures, with its appropriation of their aesthetics, with the development of "primitivism," went another sort of erasure— a double erasure, in fact: erasure of the *context* within which these objects existed, and erasure of the *circumstances* of their removal from the places where they belonged.

The African artist or sculptor from Africa or Oceania "carved in order to secure specific ends of ritual activity or to represent nature."[7] The Western view of these works was antithetical to this approach, the Western artist caring little for the ritual significance of these objects. The chance for Western art, Hal Foster argues, to "reclaim a ritual function," to "retain an ambivalence of the sacred object or gift and not be reduced to the equivalence of the commodity— was blocked."[8]

The second erasure, engendered by the concept of primitivism, was that of the barbarism, aggression, and exploitation that produced these spoils. The modernist experiment, successful as it was in art, was securely based on rape, pillage and murder, the common currency of colonial expeditions. The masks, effigies, totemic figures were all spoils of war, and nowhere is this fact ever articulated— least of all at the MOMA exhibition where the curators were interested in showing the *affinity* among the human races, and how primitivism as manifested by the modern artists is a result of this affinity. Simply put, primitivism is the result of theft.

To value as art what is now a ruin; to locate what one lacks in what one has destroyed: more is at work here than compensation... a breakthrough in our art, indeed a regeneration of our culture, is based in part on the breakup and decay of other societies... the modernist discovery of the primitive is not only in part its oblivion but its death.[9]

I started this essay by locating it within a certain event— the ROM lectures on African art, which gave an honest account of the way in which many of the ROM pieces came into its possession. It was during those lectures I heard one of the truisms that form part of the canon on African art, and one which helps to foster another type of erasure— this time about Western art. It also reveals how useful African art and primitivism have become as countercultural alternatives to Western art practices.

African art is functional, inseparable from the social order, the argument goes, vis-á-vis the Western art tradition where art by designation is what we have come to understand art to mean. Integral to this approach is the belief that art exists here in the West over and above the social order— often *apart* from the social order. The commodity value assigned to art— *and* to the artist— makes it a part of the economy, but essentially it is a thing apart— alien, alienated and, at times, alienating.

It is, however, integral to the concept and understanding of art here in the West, that its connection to the social matrix— to labour, to history and politics— not be seen, acknowledged or articulated. Which is where the African and Oceanic— the primitive— has served such a useful purpose, for with the primitive, the cultural connections between art and the social fabric— although irrevocably torn— could be clearly seen and held up as a significant difference from the Western tradition.

On the one hand, the cultural object forcibly torn out of its context, assigned artistic value and meaning, and reinterpreted as functional— an integral part of the social order; on the other, the cultural object still within its context, but with its connections to the social fabric hidden or obliterated. What are, in fact, flip sides of the same coin are presented as radical differences.

All art has its roots in social barbarism, and an "emancipatory" work of art is thus in a sense self-contradictory... Art survives by repressing the historical toil which went into its making, oblivious of its own sordid preconditions; and part of the point of radical art is to lift that repression and help us remember. We only know art because we can represent its opposite— labour.[10]

Erasure— whether we're talking of African art or Western art. For the Western consumer of art— the reader of literature as much as the gallery devotee; for the poet as much as the novelist or visual artist— that connection between art and labour, art and history or politics, between art and barbarism, has been completely erased. The consumer must see art as, at worst, neutral, at best, transcendental— existing over and above, standing over from any of the more crass aspects of our lives. For the practitioner, art is often the manifestation of the everlasting, over-worked ego, dehistoricized and existing in a vacuum.

And what of political art? It often states the obvious; becomes overly didactic in preaching to the converted; and merely serves to induce that most transitory of emotions in the liberal breast— guilt. Each person, I assume, has her own method for grappling with the utter and banal irrelevancy of art and the artist: Eagleton talks of being "popular and experimental... undermining realist [ruling class] ways of seeing"; Foster, of resisting the "commodification of culture" and constructing counter-representations. Each artist and person— if so concerned— has to find her way of resisting the erasure and amnesia— the resulting irrelevance— of art today in the West; of blowing wide open the myths and hidden assumptions— the knowledge that continues to foster the practice of forgetting.

Since I work with the written word, I see this process most clearly when I consider how LITERATURE came to the Caribbean societies. The novel, poetry, Shakespeare— all came as cultural appendages to the Empire, expressing "universal" values— the limpid objectivity of Eliot which meant that the little Black girl in the Caribbean should be able to feel exactly what he was feeling, when he wrote about cats, fog and Prufrock. And surely, that same child whose childhood boundaries were constant sunshine, black skins and mangoes could understand about Wordsworth's field of daffodils. Why the hell didn't she?

All this talk of universal values and objectivity was, of course, just so much rubbish— a carefully designed ideology to hide the fact that these art forms were very much a part of middle and upper class English life. Their export was an important aspect of empire— as important as, and probably more damaging than, colonial administrative practices.

That epitome of bourgeois art forms, the novel, whose origins, authorship and consumption lay in a class which rose to economic success and affluence on the backs of the white working class in England and the Black labouring classes in the Empire, somehow had shed all its more crass connections by the time it came south. But, as Kenyan writer Ngugi wa Thiong'o has argued, "perhaps the crucial question is not that of the racial, national, and class origins of the novel, but that of its development and the uses to which it is continually being put."[11]

Unless the artist understands that capitalist society has not only commodified the "work of art," but has also erased the barbarism which both underpins and allows the "work of art" to exist; unless the artist understands that this erasure is one of the linchpins of capitalist society which, in its own way in the West, makes art and the making of it functional, we can never begin to make the art that will challenge the hidden assumptions that support the system.

The prognosis appears bleak for artists here in the West: the split between art and labour, between art and historical under-pinnings, gape ever more widely. We may take some small hope from the integrative aspects of African creative works, as well as from the tradition in the West expressed by artists like Blake and William Morris, who saw in art an example of non-alienated labour, and, perhaps, more importantly, from the work of the many feminist artists who seek and create— admittedly often piecemeal— that integrative and, thereby, revolutionary context for their work.

I have come full circle, returning (like the objective Eliot) to where I started— the ROM, but coming from left field: why doesn't the ROM have a permanent African collection on display? Much as I abhor the history behind collections such as these, it is a grave and significant omission. It is not that the ROM doesn't have the artifacts— it does— but they're all in boxes in the basement. The ROM should either return them to the nations, tribes, and countries from which they were pilfered, give them to Africans here in Toronto or Canada, or display them. Right? But that's a whole other ball game, isn't it.

END NOTES:

1. The lecturer of this series was Jeanne Cannizzo, who subsequently guest-curated the ROM exhibit *Into the Heart of Africa*, which opened in November, 1989.

2. Christopher Hume, *Toronto Star*, April 12, 1987.

3. Daniel Mato, "Gauguin to Moore: Primitivism in Modern Sculpture," *Artmagazine*, Nov/Dec/Jan 1981-82, p. 12.

4. Hal Foster, *Primitivism in 20th Century Art: Affinity of the Tribal and the Modern.*

5. Roger Fry, *Last Lectures*, London: Cambridge University Press, 1939, p. 75.

6. Hal Foster, *Recodings: Art, Spectacle, Cultural Politics*, Port Townsend, Washington: 1985, p. 181.

7. Daniel Mato, op cit.

8. Foster, op cit.

9. Ibid.

10. Terry Eagleton, "How Do We Feed the Pagodas?" *New Statesman*, March 20, 1987, p. 8.

11. *Decolonizing the Mind*, London: James Currey, 1986, p. 68.

Museum Could Have Avoided Culture Clash

FOUR MUSEUMS, INCLUDING the Natural History Museum of Los Angeles and the Albuquerque Museum, have recently refused to stage the Royal Ontario Museum (ROM) exhibit, *Into the Heart of Africa*.

The acting director of the ROM, John McNeill, was recently quoted as saying that the "controversy which surrounded the exhibition and led to the cancellation of this tour impinges on the freedoms of all museums to maintain intellectual honesty, scientific and historical integrity and academic freedom."

With very few exceptions, all the media, print and electronic, have at one time or another echoed those opinions, and have portrayed African Canadians who challenged the ROM exhibit as being irrational, emotional and unable to grasp the irony that very quickly became the linchpin to a proper understanding of this exhibit.

The greatest irony of all, however, is that through the words of its guest curator, Jeanne Cannizzo, in the accompanying catalogue to the exhibit, the ROM had been uncannily prescient in describing the issues this show would generate. Both the ROM and the media missed this irony. The tragedy is that the ROM was unable to recognize the opportunity presented to it to do exactly what it said the show was intended to do.

Jeanne Cannizzo writes that, "[b]y studying the *museum as an artifact, reading collections as cultural texts*, and *discovering life histories of objects*, it has become possible to *understand something of the complexities of cross-cultural encounters*"[1] [my emphasis]. With these words Cannizzo, in fact, describes a framework for interpreting the exhibit and the response to it in a less adversarial way than it has been understood to date.

What follows is an analysis of the component sections of Cannizzo's statement which, had it been truly understood, could have allowed for a more informed understanding of the exhibit and the intensely negative response to it.

"*Museum as an artifact.*" For Africans, the museum has always been a significant site of their racial oppression. Within its walls reasons could be found for their being placed at the foot of the hierarchical ladder of human evolution designed by the European. Proof could also be found there of the "bizarre" nature and "primitive" anatomy of the African. Where else could you find the preserved genitalia of the black South African woman, Saarjtie Baartman, known as the "Hottentot Venus," but in the Musée de l'Homme in Paris?

The museum has been pivotal in the expansion of the West's knowledge base about the world; it has been seminal in the founding of its disciplines ethnography, archeology and anthropology; and it has been indispensable in Europe's attempt to measure, categorize and hierarchize the world with the white male at the top. And all at the expense of the African, Asian and the Native peoples, raw material for these processes.

Those who objected to the ROM's display were, in fact, showcasing the *museum as an artifact* for its uncritical and traditional presentation of these objects— the booty of soldiers and spiritual "exotica" collected by missionaries. The larger and more significant gesture of the opposition to the display lay in challenging the museum and its roles, particularly as it has affected African peoples. The potential— never realized— in this challenge was that ROM *could* find another way of looking at these objects.

"*Reading collections as cultural texts.*" The African Canadian demonstrators and other objectors *outside* the museum were, in fact, an integral and indispensable part of the cultural text *inside* the museum that Cannizzo and the ROM expressed interest in reading. In this instance, the cultural text extended beyond the walls of the museum.

The ROM argued that this was a part of Canadian life that Canadians did not know about. This immediately begs the question as to which Canadians the ROM had in mind. European or African Canadians? Or was the ROM perhaps defining "Canadian" as someone of European heritage?

This exhibit was, however, also about African history *and* African Canadians, some of whom have been here for centuries. African Canadians know the history of colonialism in a painfully intimate way; they often live its implications and repercussions every day of their lives in this country. It is, of course, a not-so-astonishing *and* racist oversight that the ROM would assume that the only meaningful audience of this exhibit would be white Canadians.

The same text resulted in contradictory readings determined by the different life histories and experiences. One reading saw these artifacts as being frozen in time and telling a story *about* white Canadian exploration of Africa; the other inserted the reader— the African Canadian reader— actively into the text, who then read those artifacts as the painful detritus of savage exploration and attempted genocide of their own people.

"*Discovering the life histories of objects.*" On one level, this collection represented a victory of the British Empire in Africa. The presence of these objects as colonial booty was, however, balanced by and resonated with that of African Canadians who represent a victory of another sort— the survival of African peoples in the New World, in the face of some five centuries of racial abuse and oppression. To discover the life histories of the objects on display, it was imperative that one also understood the *life of histories of Africans in the New World and Canada.*

Understanding the "complexities of cross-cultural encounters." What the ROM was not prepared to accept was the fact that, for the first time, a mirror was held up to its actions, and what was reflected there was an image of the museum as the cultural arm of the same powers that had exploited and continue to exploit African peoples.

The ethnographic "Other" in this case was the white Canadian fossilized in his or her bed of unconscious racism. Very much in keeping with that now notorious picture of the white missionary woman teaching African women how to wash clothes, the *cross-cultural encounter* that the curator saw as a possibility, could only happen if it went in one direction— from the repository of knowledge and power— the ROM— to the subject peoples— irrational and unsophisticated African Canadians.

And in this cacophony of racism, with its rhythms and counter-rhythms of allegation and denial, the media, while pretending to air both sides, uncritically supported the institutions of the dominant culture. African Canadians who objected to the display were, in fact, presenting a *different*, not *an inferior*, way of knowing from that of the museum "expert." For the African Canadian, those objects are still connected to them as part of an ongoing struggle against white supremacy.

In response to the controversy, Cannizzo wrote in the *Toronto Star* (June 5, 1990) that "the exhibition does not promote colonialism or glorify imperialism... it should help all Canadians understand the historical roots of racism." So what went wrong? As long as institutions and individuals fail to understand how thoroughly racism permeates the very underpinnings of Western thought, then despite all the good will in the world, catastrophes like *Into the Heart of Africa* will continue to happen. Intentions, particularly the good ones, continue to pave the way to hell. And to Africa.

The challenges to *Into the Heart of Africa* were intended to have the ROM look at these objects in another way— a way that would both reveal to white Canadians what their history has been, *as well as* support and validate the struggle of African Canadians for equality and respect, and celebrate their dynamic and astonishing survival in the New World.

Despite the recent rejections of the display by other museums, the attitude remains that those objecting to the show were wrong. If the ROM wished to show that it understood what its curator wrote in the accompanying text to the display and which I have analyzed above, it could donate a portion of the proceeds of the gate of this exhibit to helping to set up, *with African Canadian involvement*, a permanent collection of African art and artifacts in the City of Toronto, preferably under the aegis of the ROM. The ROM could also donate some of these pieces to the African Canadian community in Ontario and offer to store them on the latter's behalf. On appropriate occasions those communities could then display these pieces. Those objects are part of the cultural and spiritual patrimony of Africa and Africans that European Canadians stole, and compensation is warranted.

Gestures like these would serve to show that the ROM was beginning to understand the life histories of those objects, as well as making an attempt at a more equal cross-cultural encounter.[2]

END NOTES:

1. ROM catalogue, *Into the Heart of Africa*, p. 92.
2. In January, 1992, the ROM opened a permanent gallery on Egypt and Nubia.

Letter: January, 1990

NOW

NOW:

Did NOW sponsor trips to Germany to visit Dachau or Belsen as part of the Jewish exhibition held at the ROM a few years ago? Why then is it sponsoring safaris to Africa as part of this ROM's promotion of its recent curatorial disaster, *Into the Heart of Africa?* (A more fitting title would be *Cutting Out the Heart of Africa.*).

I can understand the ROM and the African Safari Club sponsoring this richman whiteman game, but what the hell is NOW doing sponsoring this sort of crap?

Yours truly,
M. Nourbese Philip

The "Multicultural" Whitewash

Racism in Ontario's Arts Funding System

Black artists have very little access to information regarding funding
from various arts councils, foundations or corporations.
— Black Director/Playwright

There is a need for some sensitivity and understanding for an
organization [Black theatre company] such as ours.
— Black Director

Arts councils will never allow themselves to be in a position of
being accused of not funding Black artists or groups, but it is a
question of how much. We are always asked to show how much
we expect to raise from box office receipts when we apply for
grants, yet this is not expected from groups doing summer theatre
in the parks.— Black Director

I went to see them [OAC] last year about an album— production
money— they told me they only funded the Symphony. This year I
went to them about a multicultural women's festival in Toronto

featuring music, dance and theatre. They told me they were
expecting a special grant from multiculturalism.
— Black Blues Musician

I haven't had any problems with OAC but I find the attitude
displayed by Metro Cultural Affairs condescending and patronizing.
I believe we should have permanent funding from the Secretary of
State.— Black Director

The range of possibilities in my life, I don't think that is what
people want to see about Black people... we have to have more
people who understand what we are all about... you can't afford to
have a sloppy application as a Black artist— you have to show a
lot more... you don't go in with a half-assed project because you
can't risk someone saying "we like the germ, but—"
— Black Filmmaker

THE ABOVE IS A SMALL SAMPLING of comments by Black artists in
Toronto which reflects their perceptions about funding in Ontario. Are the perceptions accurate? Are funding sources in fact
giving short shrift to Black artists from ethnic groups other than
the mainstream WASP community?

Objectivity is often an illusive goal, and only possible, I
believe, if one's biases are identified at the beginning of any
examination or analysis. My biases in this investigative piece had
to do with being a writer as well as being Black, and not
necessarily in that order. While I was interested in the arts in
general— all the arts— those requiring groups of artists, equipment, and physical space as well as those that called primarily
for solitude, being a writer meant that I was particularly sensitive
to the requirements of other artists like myself, who for the most

part work alone and need large chunks of time within which to develop their work.

Being Black meant that I was particularly interested in how Black artists were or were not being served by the various funding sources in Ontario. This could well be representative of how other artists of colour were being served.

The issue of gender was important to me as well, but concerning Black artists, the major issue that presented itself with respect to funding was race. White women appeared well, if not heavily, represented on advisory panels.

The Black artist working within her own tradition is often working across the mainstream, traditional— read white— manifestation of her chosen art form. In writing, issues having to do with dialect or standard English will arise, and if she is at all honest, so will the politics of being Black. In dance, African traditions of movement will surface; so too will the African aesthetic in painting, sculpture, or the plastic arts. The degree and intensity of the tradition, be it African or Caribbean, will naturally vary with each individual artist, but it is this element in the work of Black artists that often gets labelled "folk" or "multicultural," and contributes to some of the funding problems Black artists face. The work done by the type of Black artist I am describing here is often a challenge to, and a criticism of, the system, and must be differentiated from the "heritage" type of activity that helps to foster the myth of our happy multicultural family in Ontario.

Equipment, performance, and physical space requirements are all heavily financed in Ontario, but the individual artist who might need time to write a musical score, play or novel; the sculptor, painter or choreographer— these are severely neglected in the way the funding dollar is divided up.

[Time] is the central need, as far as creative arts are concerned, and cannot be stressed too much. Artists need time in which to conceive work, think it out, shape it, refine it, and bring it to its best fruition. They need time to think, to learn, to do research, to dream, to fill their minds with images, and then they need time to devote themselves to that curious meshing together of preconception, accident, and discipline out of which the finished work comes. They need to have no drain in their concentration, no distractions except those they seek. This is the core of it. Interpretive artists need venues, granted, but they will have nothing new or native to interpret if creative artists are robbed of the time good work requires.[1]

Because this need for time is not recognized, most artists find funding at best sporadic and modest; for the Black artist even this minimal support often appears to be nonexistent.

In Ontario there exists a range of various funding organizations at various government levels, with the OAC at the top of the heap dispensing a budget of some $27 million in its 1987 fiscal year. With the exception of those cases where artists require and receive assistance for production materials, the level and quality of funding given to individual artists is such that were all funding of them to cease, it would in no way affect their work or their commitment to it. These artists could just as well be in the *laissez faire* situation of earlier times, scrambling for individual patrons. The scramble also applies to many dance, theatre and music groups for the slim pickings available from the various funding organizations. Often sporadic and insufficient, funding often demands as much energy in pursuit of it as it does to create the work itself.

However, despite this bleak picture of funding, particularly for the individual artist, most levels of government in Ontario have now come around to accepting that, like public education or public health, there is some value in appearing to foster the arts. How or why the arts are valuable to, or should be valued by, a society has, however, not been articulated until recently.

The most clearly articulated value that policy-makers in the arts bureaucracies are now attributing to art and artists is their moneymaking potential.

"Already the cultural sector generates annual revenues of $3.5 billion in Ontario with an estimated provincial economic impact of $5.7 billion. The arts labour force is expanding at double the provincial average." So writes the Deputy Minister of Citizenship and Culture, in the *1985-86 Annual Report*. Along with this belated misunderstanding of the value of art by policy-makers in the "industry," comes an interpretation of art restricted to "big C" culture— ballet, opera, Shakespearean theatre, or symphonic music.

One result of this bottom-line approach to the arts is the general flavour permeating all funding agencies, that the artist has to justify what she is doing and why she should get paid for it— this despite all the talk about the economic potential of the arts, and despite the fact that, as the national task force on the status of the artist shows, most artists still live below the poverty line. To a lesser or greater degree, there is a basic mistrust of the artist, which has always been present in Western societies. For the Black artist who, as a Black person, encounters a general level of mistrust in this society, particularly in matters having to do with money or finance, this tradition becomes a doubly pernicious one.

The more upscale image of the arts is seen in the nurturing and fostering of "big C" culture. Culture of this sort, which many

interpret to mean "art," is seen as a means of attracting international attention— having its own opera house or symphony
allows Toronto to claim international cultural status. As a former
Executive Director of OAC has said:

The most encouraging sign— apart from the proliferating quantity
and quality of artistic work— is the interest that the business
community takes in the arts. Many corporate leaders have decided
that the arts are a priority... this means not only more corporate
money, but corporate leaders advocating on behalf of the arts to
government.
    Probably the greatest opportunities for partnership between
business and the arts are in corporate sponsorships of the
high-profile, "glamorous" arts institutions. That's the growth area.
*Where you can't expect this so much is in the avant-garde and
alternate arts, because they don't have the type of prestige that
corporations can use in the conduct of their business.*[2] [my emphasis]

    In this drive to showcase Culture, the individual artist is
forgotten and the meaning and struggle of what art is all about
is lost. It *is* about struggle and not only financial struggle; it is
about life and its twin, death; it is about politics; it is about
ordinary working people and their struggles. I could go on at
length about what I consider art to be; it is probably easier to
say what it is not: it is not what passes as Culture today in
Ontario; it is not necessarily the activities of the "Big Five" (the
Canadian Opera Company, National Ballet, Stratford Festival,
Shaw Festival, Toronto Symphony). Art can be, and often has
been, seminal in changing the way people think and feel; and

... artists have been decisive over the centuries in bringing change in the way people view the world, in nudging them to want to change it... the arts can be dangerous because they help people to think independently.[3]

There is one further wrinkle to arts funding in Ontario which relates directly to Black artists and non-Anglo-Saxon artists— the multicultural bogeyman. Ethnic groups other than Anglo- or Franco-Ontarians now comprise more than 50% of the population of Toronto. Ontario, like other provinces, has warmly clasped to its official body the concept and policies of "multiculturalism." As a concept, multiculturalism may have some validity beyond the entertainment value of Caravan, but my belief has always been that its original intent was to diffuse potential racial and ethnic problems.

In terms of arts funding, multiculturalism is the catch-all trough at which all but Ontario's Anglophone, Francophone, and Native populations must feed. In my interviews with various arts organizations, as soon as I mentioned Black artists and questioned what the agency's position was regarding the funding of art by such artists, the issue of multiculturalism would rear its head, suggesting to me that these artists, at least from the perspective of the bureaucrats, were perceived as a group apart from the artists of the dominant culture.

I make a distinction here between funding of what is called folk or heritage art— art forms such as we have come to associate with Caravan, and art which undoubtedly— as all art does— draws upon the cultural idiom of the artist, but is primarily seeking to engage with the more profound issues that all art attempts. The former has to do with maintaining tradition for tradition's sake in an alien environment, the latter with every artist's attempt to build on what their individual cultures have passed on to them, in the possibility of creating something new. If multiculturalism continues to be the official policy, and I see no evidence to indicate otherwise, heritage activities will continue to be funded by the various multicultural funding agencies. But those artists who are Black, or who do not belong to the Anglo- or Franco-Ontarian, or Native groups, and who are not merely concerned with heritage or preservation for its own sake ought, in funding matters, to be assessed along with *all other artists* in as objective a process as possible.

The major source of funding here in Ontario is the provincial government via the Ontario Arts Council (OAC), supplemented somewhat by some municipal funding from the Toronto Arts Council and Metro Cultural Affairs. Before considering these three organizations it is useful to survey some other minor funding sources in Ontario.

Universities in Ontario and Canada are not as major a source of funding for the artist as they are in the United States, and in the latter case it is usually the writer who benefits. In the U.S., universities are supported by federal, state and local governments so that the artist is, in many cases, being indirectly supported by public funds. Many universities in Ontario have writer-in-residence programmes, but otherwise universities do not subsidize artists to any extensive degree. And on the issue of race representation, to my knowledge Austin Clarke is the only Black writer who has ever held a position as writer-in-residence at an Ontario university.[4]

Libraries have also begun to become involved in writer-in-residence programmes. There are seven public library systems in Metropolitan Toronto; of these, four have writer-in-residence programmes. The competition for these positions is keen, and to my knowledge there have been no Black writers who have held this position. Admittedly, I do not know how many, if any, Black writers or writers of colour have applied, but given the selection process which is, in essence, no different from what I will outline later on, I am not sure the outcome would be any different if any or many such writers had applied.

Private foundations play a minor role in funding in Ontario, and OAC administers many endowment funds and awards including the prestigious Chalmers Fund. My personal experience with some of these private foundations— other than those administered by the OAC— may be summed up by the many pieces of unanswered correspondence I have directed their way.

With the urgency of social issues both at home and abroad— South Africa, Nicaragua, the plight of refugees— the Church has begun to play a role, albeit a small one, in funding the arts. The Canadian Catholic Organization for Development and Peace, the Anglican Church of Canada, and the United Church have all funded a small theatre group run by Black director, Amah Harris.

Harris is interested in how theatre can be used to educate young people, and has mounted shows dealing with racism, apartheid in South Africa and other issues relevant to Blacks and meaningful to all people in Toronto. She expressed scepticism about the funding practices of arts councils in relation to Black theatre groups, and instead has found churches and NGO's (Non-Governmental Organizations) very receptive to her projects and willing to provide funding. CIDA, OXFAM and CUSO are among the NGO's which have responded positively to requests for arts funding, provided the project meets their criteria of social development.

The City of Toronto, through the Toronto Arts Council and various other funding mechanisms, as well as the Cultural

Division of the Municipality of Metropolitan Toronto, otherwise known as Metro Cultural Affairs, provide further funding for Toronto artists. All told, the City of Toronto involves itself in arts funding to the tune of approximately $6 million annually, including the forgiving of rents and taxes to arts facilities, through direct grants from the Toronto Arts Council, and through a number of programmes such as the City of Toronto Book Awards, all of which are administered by various departments at City Hall.

Leaving aside, for the moment, the Toronto Arts Council, most of this funding by the City of Toronto supports arts facilities such as Massey Hall, the O'Keefe Centre and Roy Thomson Hall— in other words *high culture*, or "big C" cultural facilities. The Toronto Arts Council funds a wider spectrum of arts organizations as well as individual artists, but the trend toward mainstream funding is disturbingly similar.

As mentioned above, of the provincial arts councils, the OAC has by far the largest budget, with $27.8 million earmarked for the 1987-88 fiscal year. In addition to this sum there is another $2.25 million representing a one-time grant from the province. The Director of Special Projects at the OAC stated that this latter sum would be used to fund individual artists, either directly or indirectly, through organizations; application guidelines for this programme were slated to appear some time in late September of 1987.

The Toronto Arts Council has a budget of approximately $2.3 million and Metro Cultural Affairs will dispense some $5 million for the 1987 fiscal year. While both the OAC and the Toronto Arts Council are arms-length organizations, Metro Cultural Affairs is very much accountable to Metro Council. This means that all funding decisions made by the former must be approved by Metro Council, and politics does play a part, as it did last year over Centre Stage's production, *Spring Awakening*. Many people considered the play obscene and lobbied their municipal representatives who, in turn, brought pressure to bear on Metro Cultural Affairs.

Despite the vast differences in budgets, these three organizations— the OAC, the Toronto Arts Council, and Metro Cultural Affairs— have much in common, and are models for how arts grants are dispensed in this province. They all heavily fund the mainstream cultural groups: the OAC funds the "Big Five" to the tune of $5.8 million, and although this figure represents approximately a fifth of the OAC budget, it is assured funding. OAC's Executive Director has stated that if the Council "is going to help young artists, we have to do it while maintaining our existing organizations. We can't establish a base for the new clients by jeopardizing the base of the first group. It's tricky."[5] You bet it's tricky.

Centre Stage, Theatre Plus and Young People's Theatre receive fully half of the Toronto Arts Council budget. Three of the "Big Five," the COC, the National Ballet and the Toronto Symphony, along with the AGO receive close to 50% of Metro Cultural Affairs' budget— $2,885,000 out of $5,484,050. And many might say, so it should be.

There is another more pernicious way, however, in which these three funding organizations are similar, and that is in their absolute failure to represent the ethnic composition of Toronto and Ontario on their boards, councils, panels, and juries. These organizations cannot be accused of not ever funding Black artists or artists of colour— they have, but the question is to what degree, and how often. As Amah Harris states: "Arts councils will not place themselves in a position where they can be accused of not funding Black artists," but the quality of funding has been inadequate both in frequency and scope. Clifton Joseph, a Black dub poet in Toronto, put his experience this way: "I find it very hard to get the big money..." His experience is not unique to Black artists, artists of colour, or to the more marginalized white artists for the reasons I have been arguing throughout this article. I am also suggesting that there is a causal relationship between the composition of the various boards and committees of these funding agencies and the underfunding of Black artists and groups.

THE CHALLENGES AND IMPEDIMENTS facing the Black artist and the artist of colour force us to look at issues of high culture versus low culture; the composition of all the decision- or policy-making bodies involved in arts funding; as well as access to, and information about, funding.

My investigation of the three major funding sources in Toronto and Ontario, mentioned above, revealed them to be unrelentingly monochromatic in their make-up: white and middle class. There are some 85 ethno-cultural groups in Ontario at present, and within Toronto at least 50% of the City's residents are neither Franco- nor Anglo-Ontarian nor Native Canadian. How then do we explain the predominantly WASP nature of the OAC board, its officers and its juries? The one exception in the current list of officers is the Senior Associate Officer of the Community Arts Development Branch, dealing with Native arts, who is Japanese. One wonders at the politics of his placement in this department.

At the decision-making level of the Council the WASP factor expands exponentially. The Council makes its funding decisions in one of four ways: assessment by advisors, assessment by jury, assessment by recommendor[6] and the Formula System. The first two procedures, assessment by advisor or jury, are of most concern here, because in both these situations arts officers from each discipline select the artists or specialists who will serve as advisors or jury members.

I asked the Director of Special Projects how I would go about being selected as an advisor or a jury member: "Would I have to know the literature officer?" He agreed with me that that would be the way. Many of the working artists who belong to ethnic communities other than the dominant white community, do not socialize in circles where they would meet the officers of the arts world.

Did OAC advertise its programme or, heaven forbid, seek candidates for its juries or advisors through any of the "ethnic" newspapers? It did not. This failure to disseminate information about the nature of programmes within ethnic communities, is directly related to the issue of access, or lack thereof, mentioned earlier. There has been no attempt made by this organization, which dispenses some $27 million of the taxpayers' dollars, to represent the ethnic composition of the province or the different and differing arts communities which it is set up to serve.

However, the OAC *is* in the process of setting up a multicultural department. A Committee has already been struck comprised of staff members, Council members, and some community representatives. Who these community representatives are; which communities they represent; why Black artists in Toronto know nothing about this; and why this development was not advertised in the "ethnic" presses, are questions that still remain unanswered.

More substantive concerns revolve around issues such as the need for a separate multicultural department at all. The Director of Special Projects suggested that there was precedent for such a department in the model of the current Franco-Ontario depart-ment. Would the new department be expected to serve the many artists from the 85 ethno-cultural groups? And would its mandate be to fund heritage/preservation projects *as well as* art anchored in a specific cultural heritage but seriously exploring and creating something new? These are hard questions and they ought to be addressed thoroughly through briefs and public discussions. The Director told me he believed discussions would include the public, after the Council committee had finished its discussions.

I would far rather see the Council increase its budget in all the arts disciplines; make the decision-making process more equitable for *all* artists, and raise its profile among artists in non-Anglo-Saxon communities, so that those artists have better access to the information, than have another multicultural fund set up from which all those "other" artists will have to seek assistance.

Whether or not public hearings are held about the portended multicultural department, the OAC must be challenged on its lack of representation of the artists it serves, and the Ministry of Citizenship and Culture held accountable for these practices. On the question of the Ministry's policies relating to the issues of culture and multiculturalism, an officer of the same Ministry had this to say: "While looking at cultural issues we are also looking at issues concerning multiculturalism. It is easy to overlook this because of the hybrid nature of the issue." So much for policy. When asked about an OAC administered competition, "Writer's Reward," to choose a book promoting an understand-ing of Ontario and its citizens through their work, in response to the questions *which* Ontario and *which* citizens, he replied that Ontario was "quintessentially a multicultural community," but pointed out that some of our best writers like Alice Munro and Robertson Davies had won acclaim for their recreation of small-town Ontario life. While Ontario may be described as a "multicultural" province, this multicultural experience is to be found primarily in urban areas. However, neither the OAC, the Toronto Arts Council nor Metro Cultural Affairs— all of which are city-based— reflect the officer's description of Ontario as a "quintessentially multicultural community." They represent, in fact, the cultural and racial homogeneity of small-town Ontario.

METRO CULTURAL AFFAIRS, WHICH ONLY funds incorporated groups, works on a panel system once an application has been accepted. Funding covers all disciplines except literature. I had made an appointment to interview the Director of the programme, but was not surprised when I got to City Hall and was told that she was unavailable. I met instead with two officers whose job it was to help applicants prepare their applications for the appropriate panels. When I raised the issue of Black artists and artists of colour, they immediately told me that they did have a multicultural and race relations branch. This department which has a budget of some $300,000, in fact, funds *no* arts activities except for the odd heritage-type activity.

In response to my question concerning the selection of panel members, I was told that the Director "does research and gets names from granting agencies for people (not necessarily artists) who would be suitable." Again the exponential WASP factor. All panel members are paid, as is the case with OAC jury members and advisors. I asked for the list of the 1987 panel members: all were white and represented the mainstream arts culture.

Prior to my interview with Metro Cultural Affairs, I myself

had been approached by the Director to write a review of a Black Theatre Canada (BTC) production, *Under Exposure*. BTC is funded by Metro Cultural Affairs, and my suspicions were aroused that there was more to the request than a mere review. This was later borne out by my discovery that Metro Cultural Affairs and BTC have had a running feud over funding ever since the appointment of the current Director. My honorarium for this review— a generous one— was $50.00. I only mention this incident to show that when Black artists are sought out to make critical assessments or judgements, it is often because those seeking their skills want to validate a negative decision regarding a Black group or artist.

Regarding the issue of gender, though, the officers assured me that they did try to get a balance: the 1987 panel list reveals there were seven men and six women. I dare say we ought to be grateful for small mercies.

The 1987 Toronto Arts Council Grants Report and Recommendation states that the arts "express and enhance our *unique ethnic diversity...*" [my emphasis]— an ethnic diversity that is appallingly absent from the membership of the Toronto Arts Council and its committees. Under "Method of Evaluation" the same report states that,

Each committee is chaired by a member of the Toronto Arts Council Board; together they have representation from a *wide range of the arts community*. All committee members are volunteers with extensive professional experience in their fields. [my emphasis]

I felt that the latter description fitted me so I asked the Executive Director how I could get on to the literary committee.

"Committee members are chosen by the committee," she told me, therefore unless I knew a committee member... the script was the same, and the list of committee members for literature— June Callwood, Kass Banning, Carol Bolt, Susan Crean, etc.— confirmed my expectations.

As was the case with the OAC and Metro Cultural Affairs, there was no advertisement of their programme or of committee vacancies in any of the "ethnic" newspapers. But there was a Special Events and Festival Committee— read *multicultural*— and, yes, there was one Black person— Ayanna Black— on this committee; on the Toronto Arts Council board there was one Japanese member, Raymond Moriyama, an architect.

The "quintessential multicultural community"; a community of "unique ethnic diversity," to quote the Toronto Arts Council itself, and yet this diversity, this multiculturalism, these quintessential qualities were nowhere to be found in three organizations that between them dispense some $36 million of taxpayers' money.

Secretary of State funding of multicultural projects is instructive in so far as it demonstrates some of the potential problems for artists seeking assistance from a fund with a multicultural mandate.

The officer in charge of funding applications at the Secretary of State multicultural department made it clear that the department supported the "development of ethno-cultural artistic expression." The department was not only interested in the technical or formal expression of the art in question, but also in the message. This message should be a prescriptive one which would move the community in question closer to integration into Canadian society; multiculturalism is therefore interpreted as a stepping stone to greater integration.

The department funds groups and individuals and the officer was unequivocal in his expression of their preference for projects with a social change aspect. "Excellence"— a word bandied about by various arts councils— technical or otherwise, is not their main focus. Their budget, however, is not a large one— $23-24 million nationally, compared with $27 million dispensed by the OAC for Ontario alone.

The Black artist is very often caught between a rock and a hard place. It may appear, on the surface at least, that the Secretary of State, or any multicultural fund for that matter, may be more receptive to her work. However, there are very clear guidelines as to what "multiculturalism" ought to mean in this society. If that aspect or interpretation is missing from the work in question, the artist will not be funded— even under a multicultural mandate.

I do not for one moment believe that it will be any easier for Black artists, or artists of colour, or "ethnic" artists to get grants from the OAC's multicultural department, if and when it is set up, unless their work conforms to whatever the official multi-cultural ideal is.

Systems or practices which may appear to be neutral and which may be implemented impartially, but which operate to exclude women and other racial groups.

So reads the definition of systemic discrimination as described in the Study of the Recruitment and Advancement Policies and Practices in the Ontario Civil Service.[7] It continues,

There is no single policy or procedure which, itself, can be said to be the key to systemic discrimination... it is the cumulative effect of the various policies and practices and the enabling measures which result in perceived and actual instances of discrimination.

One of the more pernicious practices identified by this study which helps to entrench systemic discrimination is word-of-mouth recruiting. Networking is inevitable and at times desirable in any community: it provides an easy informal way of moving information around a group. However, publicly funded groups such as the OAC and Toronto Arts Council and even Metro Cultural Affairs, because of its non arms-length relationship with Metro Council, must strive to make their staffs, boards and advisors representative of the artists and artists' groups in this province. That means the WASP factor has to be balanced by individuals from other ethnic groups.

It is very clear that within these organizations, there is no value placed on having their entire organization, including staff, panels and juries, reflect the racial and ethnic diversity that exists in the population, as well as in the various arts groups and among individual artists in Ontario.

One often-reiterated complaint among Black artists is the lack of access to information about the various funding programmes. Many of these artists are forced to rely on artist-run centres such as A Space to obtain the information they want. All these artist-run centres are white, but without them many Black artists, particularly in the visual arts or theatre, would have even less access to information on funding.

These centres sponsor many of these artists, thereby enabling them to get public funding second-hand. I haven't heard any criticism of these artist-run centres with respect to Black artists, but as one artist has pointed out to me, any Black activity sponsored by these centres is but one of many programmes— it is not the focus of the centre. There are no Black artist-run centres. Black director, Ahdri Zhina Mandiela, attributes this lack to the chronic financial difficulty Black artists face. In order to qualify for funding, artist-run centres have to have been in existence for a minimum period of time, which in turn requires some independent source of financing which most Black artists do not have.

There are, however, some very simple, straightforward ways arts organizations can begin to deal with systemic discrimination and their failure to deliver services to Black artists and artists of colour:

1. Advertise funding programmes in the "ethnic" presses and newsletters.
2. Advertise vacancies on panels and juries in these presses.
3. Contact publishers, magazines, art galleries or other arts organizations who have contacts with artists in various ethnic groups and have them supply names of candidates for vacant positions on advisory panels.
4. Reduce the extensive word-of-mouth recruitment for advisory panels.

Bureaucracies, arts organizations notwithstanding, have never been known for their willingness to adopt simple solutions, and I am certainly not holding my breath about changes, but as one dub poet put it: "The bottom line is we've got to get some of that cash— it is taxpayers' money and we're entitled to some of it."

This article has attempted two things: to wrestle with some of the more fundamental problems regarding funding for the individual artist, pink, yellow, blue, black or white; and to reveal some aspects of the systemic racism permeating the arts funding system. I have argued that systemic racism has shown itself in two ways: 1) in the failure to communicate news of funding programmes to the various communities which the arts councils are intended to serve, and 2) in a closely-knit virulent type of networking that ensures the selection of one particular kind of artist, specialist or person to serve on arts councils or funding agencies. There are two aspects to the latter issue— one is the *visible* composition of the board and councils, as well as the advisory panels which fail to represent the ethnic mix in Ontario. The other aspect is ensuring that panel members understand the cultural idioms in which some of the applicants— such as Black artists— are working.

At present, many artists— Black artists— believe that it is futile for them to apply for funding; they do not believe their applications will be considered fairly. And they are right: if they are working in an idiom that is unknown to panel advisors, such as dialect or dub, how can that work be assessed fairly? One artist told me that an application he sent to the Canada Council was returned with the supporting material unopened. Another— a Black director— said that her work is described as "folk" because of its context, and "lacking professionalism" because of its rough quality. She doesn't deny the rough quality, but asserts that it is directly related to financial constraints— rehearsal time for artists, space and equipment rental— all of which are related to the issue of accessibility of funding.

Funding awards to Black artists may not necessarily increase if the funding agencies become more representative, both in terms of their visible composition, as well as the understanding and grasp, by panel members, of cultural idioms other than the mainstream white traditions. If nothing else, however, these agencies will be perceived as being less partial in their decision-making process. Black artists will then be able to believe they have as good a chance as other applicants at getting a grant.

ART IS NOT A JOB; art is work... The nature of artistic work is *vocational*, the diametrical opposite of *employment*. This is not understood by policy-makers; if it were we would not have comments such as that made by the Deputy Minister of Culture about the "arts labour force." "What labour force? Where is it located? Who is its employer?" If the Deputy Minister really meant what he said, we should all be put on the payroll as the Independent Artists Union demands.

The current view of art is that the arts are a money-making venture; there is yet no evidence that funding bureaucrats understand the potential of art to heal, ennoble, change— to galvanize individuals and societies to make changes. Even though most of the Black artists working in Ontario have their immediate roots in the New World, their heritage is an African one which considers the artist's role in the community to be spiritual and integrative. Mistrust of and contempt for the artist are alien to African traditions. Ontario's treatment of its Black artists, as well as many of its non-Black artists, only serves to set the artist at further odds with the community. The artist's loss, however, is also the community's.

Most of the artists I know write, paint, sculpt or film despite the lack of funding; funding plays a minimal, if any, role in their lives. They all "catch as catch can" (make do with what you have and take opportunities as they arise), working at various odd jobs while continuing to practise their chosen discipline. They are not a "labour force," but they do labour exceedingly hard at what they do. They don't keep regular hours yet manage to get their rent and Ma Bell paid. However, I doubt we will make any advances beyond the pecuniary if we are co-opted into the brave new world of corporate financing, or are forced to show how our art can pay its way. Sometimes art's most profound claim is that it does *not* pay its way, yet maintains an astonishing validity in today's world.

Material deprivation, lack of money and security become scourges for many, if not most, artists; poverty only serves to embitter the artist and may even poison her work. Security often guarantees the production of the very best work possible. The individual artist in Ontario, however, particularly the Black artist who, in some ways, is representative of all those artists who are not part of the white mainstream, has to look to sources other than funding for her security. In this "quintessentially multi-cultural province," such security is still a long way off.

It will remain that way while the two-tiered and, yes, racist practice of funding remains in Ontario. In essence what it all means is that Ontario is accumulating among its artists a considerable reserve of hostility, resentment and anger, as well as a sense of outsidership. Artists often foster this feeling among themselves, but I am not sure it is a policy to recommend itself to governments. Eventually it means rebellion, resistance and conflict, particularly in a society so steeped in racism, and one that sees a widening gap between those who have and those who do not.

Accepting, as I do, the power of art to catalyze and change things, it is only a matter of time before these things come together and someone, somewhere, begins demanding more radical, immediate change. More important than this possibly empty prediction is the fact that art and artists are the repository of tremendous spiritual power in any society— for all its people;

art's practice often demands tremendous sacrifices from those who are called to be artists, and so when the official policies of a society suggest that the artist and her work are invalid, or valueless— for whatever reason— then the whole society loses. The artist is probably the stronger for it, for sometimes it appears that the only quality required is sheer brute determination in the face of all odds. But the society loses, as Toronto and Ontario have already lost, in their failure to draw on the talents of some of the finest artists working at their art today.

END NOTES:

1. Les Murray, *The Peasant Mandarin*, University of Queensland Press, 1978.
2. *n.b.*, Number 1, Ontario Arts Council, p. 4.
3. John Calder, "Art and the Tories," *New Statesman*, 17.
4. Since the writing of this piece, in 1987, I am aware of one other Black writer who has held a writer-in-residence position at an Ontario university.
5. *n.b.*, op cit.
6. The OAC funds its writers through the recommendor system. The system is, in theory, a fairly enlightened one since all that is required is for the publisher to recommend the writer for a grant, without the need for an extensive description of the project. However, young or beginning Black writers and writers of colour seldom know white or mainstream publishers. Of the three presses who have openly expressed a commitment to publish work by Black writers, only one qualifies for OAC grants. Publishers also tend to spread these grants fairly thinly, giving many writers small amounts of money; some have even been known to demand kickbacks for recommending writers.
7. Avebury Research and Consulting Ltd.

Disturbing the Peace

... it is true that the nature of society is to create, among its citizens, an illusion of safety; but it is also absolutely true that the safety is always necessarily an illusion. Artists are here to disturb the peace.— James Baldwin

DISTURBING THE PEACE. That was what a small group of writers, artists and supporters were doing outside Roy Thomson Hall on the evening of September 24, 1989. We were "disturbing the peace" by leafletting the guests as they attended the Gala of the 54th PEN Congress. To describe us as an odd bunch would not have been amiss. We comprised an Anglo-Canadian teen-aged student doing a project on racism and writing; a South African refugee; an African Canadian employee of The Women's Press; a Chinese Canadian playwright; an Anglo-Canadian adult educator; an Asian Canadian writer; two Anglo-Canadian volunteers from the rape crisis centre; an African Canadian writer and critic; an Anglo-Canadian writer and critic; an Irish Canadian writer; and myself, an African Canadian of Caribbean background.[1]

Some of us were members of a fledgling group, *Vision 21: Canadian Culture in the 21st Century*, which had been formed in July, 1989, around issues of multicultural representation, racism and the arts. Some were members of Multicultural

Women Writers of Canada, a group formed in May, 1989, in response to the failure of the Writers' Union to deal with issues of racism and sexism.

The more immediate context to our presence outside Roy Thomson Hall on the evening of September 24, 1989, reached back some eighteen months to the split of The Women's Press over the issue of racism in writing and publishing. The debate generated by these events swirled in the media as well as the writing community for many months, only to surface once again at the Annual General Meeting (AGM) of the Writers' Union in May, 1989. At this meeting, certain members of the Union brought a motion to set up a task force to look into racism in writing and publishing in Canada; the motion failed to carry, leading to no little debate and even dissension.

These events were but the high points to a long-standing struggle on the part of many artists and writers across Canada, against racism and its manifestations, both in the various disciplines of art and in the structures managing these disciplines, such as arts councils and associations. The face-off between the League of Canadian Poets and De Dub Poets several years earlier was one of the more notorious manifestations of this reality. Prior to that there was the *Fireweed* issue, edited by women of colour, which dealt with these issues. Makeda Silvera's address at the 1983 Women and Words Conference also raised the issue of racism. In writing and publishing in Canada, racism was by no means a new issue.

As a poet and writer, my own personal involvement in and contribution to this struggle has primarily been as a critic and writer, always attempting, in the words of James Baldwin, to disturb the peace of those invested in maintaining the status quo.

The aim of this involvement has always been to articulate the
nature of racism in the arts, to reveal the profound injustices that
result from the systemic practice of racism, and to push those
who try to manage and diffuse the effects of this practice, to
respond to the legitimate needs and demands of African Canadian writers and artists in Canada. Based on this involvement,
there was, in fact, a certain inevitability to my standing outside
Roy Thomson Hall, along with fellow artists and supporters,
holding signs and placards and giving out leaflets that challenged
PEN Canada for locking out writers of colour, and thereby using
up our fifteen minutes of Warholian fame.

The fundamental purpose to our leafletting campaign was,
and always had been, to advance the state of the debate concerning racism and the arts here in Canada. Our aim was not to
change PEN Canada or PEN International. We merely used the
ethnic and racial composition of the Canadian contingent as a
startling yet predictable example of the official face of racism in
the arts in Canada. None of the individuals demonstrating
outside Roy Thomson Hall wanted to be invited to participate
in the 54th PEN Congress. What we did want to do, however,
was bring to the attention of *all* PEN delegates, both from
Canada and from abroad, the fact that there was and is a very
real problem with racism in writing and publishing here in
Canada which, in many instances, serves to silence African,
Asian, and First Nations writers. We argued in our leaflet (see
appendix below) that such silencing of writers, while in no way
equivalent to the imprisonment of a writer, was serious enough
to warrant the attention of an organization such as PEN and the
delegates to the Congress.

There was an unusual lack of pre-publicity about the 54th

PEN Congress; however, in the week immediately prior to the Congress, NOW *Magazine* published a schedule which revealed that most of the writers and moderators comprising the Canadian delegation were white. The schedule also mentioned "Next Generation" readings, but the individuals taking part in this event were unnamed.

Our first response to this schedule was a letter to NOW *Magazine* (September 21, 1989) signed by myself, Kass Banning, Cameron Bailey, Winston Smith, and Enid Lee, protesting the under-representation of writers of colour at the Congress. During that week there was much discussion about whether we should do anything further, and if so what the best plan would be. Because of lack of time and bodies, we eventually decided that the best approach was that of leafletting. The leaflet we designed provided information to delegates about racism in writing and publishing in Canada: it gave a background to the issue by outlining the official policy of multiculturalism and the latter's relationship to racism, as well as describing the more recent events in writing and publishing relating to these issues. Through the leaflet we welcomed the presence of "Third World" writers in Canada, and supported PEN's work on behalf of imprisoned writers. However, we also pointed out the peculiar form of silencing of writers that takes place in Canada as a consequence of racism, and drew attention to the overwhelmingly white, Anglo-Saxon, Protestant (WASP) composition of the Canadian delegation as an example of this racism. We argued that this was tantamount to the exclusion of Black writers and writers of colour. We asked delegates to raise these issues in their panels.

Unaware that there was a reception (courtesy of *Saturday*

Night) being held prior to the concert, we arrived at Roy Thomson Hall on the evening of September 24, 1989, only to find that many of the delegates had already entered the Hall, although we had allowed ourselves at least 45 minutes to leaflet. However, we were still able to leaflet a number of guests as they entered the Hall.

Some guests supported us, others quite clearly disapproved of us, and still others stopped to argue with us, challenging us to prove our "allegations." The most common objection we heard was that it was "inappropriate" for us to be there— read impolite, this is Canada eh! That appropriateness had become one of the trappings of democracy, was a revelation to me that evening. At the end of that stint of leafletting we all felt exhilarated and believed that despite missing many of the delegates and guests, we had accomplished something.

We returned after the concert to leaflet the guests we had missed on their way in, and found very much the same responses among the departing guests as there were earlier. Some guests, having sat through the concert, now agreed with our interpretation of the event; others asked for bookstores where they could find the books of the writers of colour; there were also those who continued to disapprove of us. One guest even pointed to a typographical error in the leaflet and, with great malice, said that since we couldn't spell we could not be taken seriously.

By about 11 p.m., our already small group had dwindled to about five or six tired but satisfied leafletters. We were collecting our signs preparatory to leaving, when we noticed two people coming through the front doors of Roy Thomson Hall. I approached the couple and, as I had done on many, many occasions that evening, held out a leaflet to the woman who preceded her companion. I do not recall that I even had a chance to say what I had customarily been saying to guests— "Have you had one of these?" The woman's response was swift as it was vicious.

"Fuck off!" she said to me. That woman was June Callwood, the then incoming President of PEN Canada. Sheelagh Conway— a member of Multicultural Women Writers of Canada— who was standing next to me, told Mrs. Callwood that she ought to be ashamed of herself for what she had just said, to which the latter once again replied, "fuck off." As she passed the other members of the group (some three or four people who were merely sitting quietly), June Callwood once again told us to "fuck off." During the course of that entire evening, June Callwood had been the only person who responded in such an abusive manner. The irony is that as President of PEN Canada, June Callwood is head of an organization whose members are sworn to uphold freedom of speech, particularly for writers, the world over.

Contrary to the *Globe and Mail* article (Tuesday, September 26, 1989), no member of our group accosted anyone that evening, including June Callwood. We were a small, low keyed group of people who merely handed out leaflets. Occasionally the odd voice or voices would be raised in a chant challenging PEN to "do the right thing." Contrary to the *Globe and Mail* editorial of September 27, 1989,[2] ("PEN Pals"), June Callwood was not "tormented" by anyone, nor was there a "heated altercation." Altercation suggests at least two people engaged in discourse. No one said anything to June Callwood before she abused us. Contrary to the suggestion in the September 30, 1989, *Globe and Mail* piece by Bronwyn Drainie, no one drove

June Callwood to obscenities or profanity. Her verbal attack on us, for that was what it was, was unprovoked and unwarranted.

June Callwood said "fuck off" in public and thereby used up *her* fifteen minutes of Warholian fame. In that her profanity and abuse garnered Vision 21 more media attention for its issues, her response, albeit personally distasteful to me, could be seen to be helpful.

However, because Callwood is an iconic representation of liberalism in Canada, the media, after the immediate news coverage, rushed to find excuses for her abuse of us. As mentioned above, use of words like "accost," "tormentor" and "heated altercation" was prevalent, and in a more recent article the *Toronto Sun* described us as a "gang." These are all examples of damage control on behalf of Callwood by the media.

In the more extreme cases such as the *Globe and Mail* editorial and the *Sun* piece, there was also an attempt to discredit us and our arguments about racism in Canada.

The reason for Callwood's response to us, however, is not hard to find. In a *Marxism Today* (August, 1989) article on racial turmoil between British Muslims and English people in Bradford, journalist Simon Reyell writes that there is a "fundamental intolerance which ordinarily lurks beneath the surface 'as long as they keep themselves to themselves,' [which] erupts whenever a minority culture impinges on the day-to-day life of the majority culture." And that was what June Callwood's "fuck off" was all about— minority culture impinging on majority culture. In the media's rush to protect her, however, the legitimate issues concerning racism in Canada have tended to be discredited along with us as individuals. The corollary of this is that responsible media coverage, both of the issues we raised and June Callwood's response, has been virtually non-existent.

MEDIA COVERAGE

THE *TORONTO STAR* GAVE the leafletting and demonstration a few lines in its September 25, 1989, issue. It did not mention the event again, nor did it mention the Callwood incident. It did, however, in a later piece (*Toronto Star*, October 2, 1989) refer, in terms very disparaging to Sheelagh Conway, to an interaction between her and Betty Friedan, that took place on Wednesday, September 27, 1989, at Union Station.

CBC radio carried the item about the demonstration and Callwood's profanity twice on the morning of Monday, September 25, 1989, on its *On the Arts* program. Significantly, in its September 29, 1989, *Morningside* coverage and summing up of the events in Toronto, and the train trip to Montreal, there was no mention made of the leafletting campaign or Callwood's abuse of the individuals handing out leaflets.

The Village Voice, in its November, 1989, Literary Supplement, described us as "local writers from the immigrant community" who were picketing "alleged racism." The article conceded that "the protesters had a point"; that "the [Canadian] mosaic... could have been more variously represented," and suggested that we "could have been invited to attend the Congress as observers."

Neither *Share* nor *Contrast*, the two newspapers serving the African Canadian community in Toronto and with whom I spoke, took any interest in the issue, nor did they cover the leafletting, or the issue of Callwood's response to us.

Surprisingly, however, the *Globe and Mail* was the exception to the studied indifference of the media, and the only organ of the media, print or otherwise, mainstream or marginal, that gave the demonstration any reasonable coverage or treated it with the

seriousness it warranted (Tuesday, September 26, 1989). Report-
ers H.J. Kirchhoff and Isabel Vincent must be given credit for
this. However, the *Globe* editorial of the following day, "PEN
Pals," did an impressive job of damage control; in its tone, it
attempted to make light of June Callwood's behaviour, euphe-
mistically referring to Callwood's abuse as an "Anglo-Saxon
expletive." Clearly, the editorial's intent was to excuse her actions
by suggesting we were at fault.

NOW *Magazine* was helpful in allowing us to deliver two
letters to them after their deadline; beyond that they gave no
coverage of any of the events we had been involved in, nor did
they in any of their articles deal specifically with the issue of
racism which we raised.

TVOntario, the publicly funded television channel, on its
Imprint show (September 9), featured Graeme Gibson and June
Callwood who, in discussing the issue of our leafletting the Gala,
suggested that we were witch-hunting; that we were not writers
and that we had not done our homework. TVO did not, as it
ought to have done, provide us with an opportunity to put
forward our position or to rebut the inaccurate statements that
were being made.

The media have, in fact, effectively censored the expression
of our views concerning the composition of the Canadian
delegation to the 54th Congress, as well as the events that took
place outside Roy Thomson Hall. Whether or not this was
intentional is irrelevant. The result of this censorship has been
protection of the image— I am tempted to say the illusion— of
Canada as a non-racist, and in the words of Graeme Gibson,
the then President of PEN Canada, an "indecently rich Third
World country."

The irony of all this is that the explicit mandate of PEN

Canada and PEN International is the opposition of censorship wherever it occurs. Clearly, the maintenance of a certain image is far more important to the media than the significance of Callwood's abusive response to our very small demonstration against racism. The cumulative result of this approach is, once again, a complete denial of the existence of racism in Canada and a dismissal of the issue.

AFTERMATH

AS REPRESENTATIVES of Multicultural Women Writers of Canada and Vision 21 respectively, Sheelagh Conway and I called on June Callwood to take responsibility for her actions and to apologize for swearing at us. In a letter to the *Globe and Mail* on September 29, 1989, I personally called upon her to apologize to me for her abuse. We have also called for her resignation as President of PEN Canada. To date there has been no response from her. Her silence speaks more than the clichéd volumes.

On the morning of September 26, 1989, the morning on which the first *Globe and Mail* piece appeared, I received an anonymous phone call from a male calling me "nigger." I do not and cannot hold June Callwood responsible for this reprehensible type of behaviour. I do, however, believe that when individuals of her stature in this country take a dismissive approach to issues of racism, sinking to the level of profanity; when a *Globe and Mail* editorial excuses this attitude with euphemistic platitudes and patent inaccuracies, the result is a climate in which this more extreme type of behaviour begins to surface.

Callwood has been quoted as saying she was "outraged" (*Globe and Mail*, September 26, 1989) that we had "got our facts wrong," and that we hadn't "done our homework." Surely, her response— as incoming President of PEN, with access to the facts— ought to have been one in which she demonstrated *how* we had gotten our facts wrong. Instead, what we got was something very close to the verbal equivalent of the Chinese government to its demonstrators in Tiananmen Square.

Subsequent "corrections" of our "wrong facts" by John Ralston Saul, then Secretary of PEN Canada, stated that "more than 20 Canadian writers of minority or ethnic background participated" (the *Globe and Mail*, September 28, 1989). These figures have since been adjusted downward to give us the most recent and final "correction" of our facts, (the *Globe and Mail*, October 2, 1989), "At least five of the congress' 51 invited Canadian guests were 'ethnic,'" or as many as 10 or 12, depending on how you figured it. This would be entirely risible if it weren't so serious.

The Ontario government now has in place policies which make a distinction between multiculturalism, which deals with *all* ethnic minorities, and race relations, which address the issue of race and colour, a distinction which appears to have escaped those involved in the *Globe and Mail* pieces mentioned in the previous paragraph. Vision 21's leaflet identified five or at most seven writers of colour.[2] I had always understood the phrase "writer of colour" to have a specific meaning— those writers who are not white. It is a catch-all and therefore, at times, inaccurate phrase including, but not exclusively, African, Asian and Native writers. While we raised the issue of ethnicity in our leaflet, our arguments were directed primarily at racism affecting African, Asian and Native writers in Canada, as exemplified by their under-representation at the Congress. Nothing in the "corrections" of our facts in any way contradicted what we observed and had noted about the composition of the Canadian delegation to the 54th Congress— that it contained five and possibly seven writers of colour.

The emphasis laid by many spokespersons for PEN Canada subsequent to our leafletting, on the presence of writers from developing countries, exemplifies a particularly pernicious form of Canadian internationalism, which promotes Canada as an international do-gooder while, as in this instance, practising a racism at home as virulent as any found in the U.S. Neither is this fork-tongued practice restricted to issues of racism. Canada's handling of the South African situation is symptomatic of this behaviour: while talking about the need for sanctions against South Africa, Canadian trade with that country increased dramatically. While mouthing platitudes about human rights violations, Canada, under the guise of private enterprise (Armx), hosted a major arms fair (Spring, 1989) that welcomed many of those very countries (with the exception of Eastern block countries) that Canada condemned for human rights violations. The presence of writers of colour from overseas and from developing countries at the 54th Congress was intended, and is now being used, as an answer to a critique of Canadian racism practised against African, Asian, and First Nations Canadian writers. It is not, nor can it ever be, an acceptable answer.

We Canadians live in a society where racism permeates the very fabric; the arts, and in this case writing and publishing are in no way immune to this particular problem. Like an alcoholic who will not accept that he or she has a drinking problem, Canada cannot be helped until it accepts there is a problem. The response to our leafletting and demonstration by June Callwood and the media (except for the *Globe and Mail*'s initial piece) is an example of this dissimulation and self-delusion.

There is a vast chasm that presently exists between the rhetoric of politicians who chorus the existence of a multicultural, multi-racial society, and the reality for African, Asian and Native Canadians in this society. And rhetoric it will remain as long as organizations such as PEN Canada fail to turn that rhetoric into something more substantial. We have come to expect rhetoric from politicians, but the existence of that rhetoric usually means that the politician is responding to a felt need in the society. It behooves organizations to respond to those needs. Many government agencies, organizations, and departments funded the 54th PEN Congress. One would have thought that ministries like the Ministry of Culture and Communications would have insisted that before being able to obtain funding, the Canadian delegation reflect the make-up of this province and country. This did not happen and PEN Canada was able, with the assistance of public funds, to put together a Canadian delegation that was fundamentally non-representative of Canada's peoples.

Small as it was, I believe our group accomplished what it set out to do, although I *am* aware that there is a personal cost to this— the bringer of bad news is seldom, if ever, welcomed. Our intention was to conscientize the larger society to the presence of racism in writing and publishing here in Canada, *and* to advance the debate on racism in those areas. Already, I have seen changes that are the direct outcome of our work around the 54th PEN Congress.

James Baldwin argues that our role as artists is to disturb the peace, and this is not only, or necessarily, in the political sense. What we were doing on Sunday, September 24, 1989, was, I believe, a natural outcome of our lives as artists committed to creating a more equitable world in which the practice of our art

can continue; our actions reflected, in fact, a profound commitment to this country, its future and the future of our children.

As artists, we must continue to disturb the peace in whatever
ways we are most comfortable. For some of us it might mean
living the most honest life possible, a difficult thing in today's
world; for others, in a society that seems so satisfied with
mediocrity, it might mean writing as excellently as possible. For
still others it might mean becoming more active, if only tempo-
rarily.

The peace Baldwin refers to often means the status quo,
controlled and/or legalized oppression, or a self-satisfied smug-
ness so prevalent in Canada. When peace means those things,
not to disturb it means to collude with it. The writer has an
obligation not only to disturb but even to destroy that sort of
peace.

Appendix I

PEN Canada Locks Out Writers of Colour

IN-VISIBLE INK: CANADA

1. Canada is a multi-racial, multi-ethnic society. Multiculturalism is the official
policy of the governments of Canada, Ontario and Metropolitan Toronto.
2. At its lowest common denominator, multiculturalism means the equal access
of all ethnic, cultural and racial groups to the resources that the Canadian
society has to offer.
3. Contrary to the policy of multiculturalism there is a dominant culture in
Canada which is white, middle class and Anglo-Saxon. Racism, in fact,
permeates all aspects of Canadian life including writing and publishing.

WRITING AND PUBLISHING IN CANADA

1. African, Asian and Native Canadian writers are consistently underfunded by
arts councils; publishers are reluctant to publish their works, and when
published, their works are often ignored by reviewers.
2. Some Native Canadian writers have also expressed concern about the use of
their myths, legends and tales by white writers, while their own work remains
unpublished.
3. The Writers' Union of Canada is an organization which purports to
represent most of the writers in Canada today. Its role is to represent writers
and advocate on their behalf. Membership of the Union is almost entirely white.
4. In September, 1988, the Union censored the resignation statement of a
female member relating to the presence of sexism within the Union

membership, by disallowing publication of this statement in the Union newsletter.

5. In May, 1989, at the Annual General Meeting of the Writers' Union, the Union refused to look at the issue of racism in Canadian publishing and writing.

6. A significant number of the Canadian organizers of PEN Canada are also members of the Writers' Union.

The 54th PEN CONGRESS

1. Fifty-one Canadians are scheduled to take part in the 54th PEN Congress at Harbourfront, Toronto. Only seven of these participants are Asian, African or Native Canadian. There is also a marked dearth of Canadians from ethnic backgrounds which are not English.

2. The overwhelming majority of the white Canadian participants reflects what is, in fact, the dominant culture of Canada— white, middle class, and Anglo-Saxon.

3. These latter writers all appear in events for which an admission fee is charged; with the exception of one Black and one Native writer, all other Canadian writers of colour have been scheduled to participate in panels or readings described as Next Generation events, all of which are free.

4. In the two years PEN Canada has had to organize this event, its organizers have made no attempt to involve writers of colour. There have, for instance, been no membership drives among such writers, the result of which is the overwhelmingly white membership of PEN Canada, which is in turn reflected in Canada's representation at the 54th Congress.

5. While the numerical representation of women at the congress is an accurate reflection of Canadian society, this representation is, however, overwhelmingly white, middle class and Anglophone.

FREEDOM AND POWER

While the presence of writers from Asia, Africa, the Caribbean and Latin America is a welcome one, when these writers leave, African, Asian and Native Canadian writers continue to face the implacable face of racism in writing and publishing here in Canada.

While we appreciate our relative freedoms here in the West, freedoms which are, at best, limited, we also wish to point out that freedom and power can be effectively and efficiently curtailed without the physical imprisonment of a writer. If the so-called freedom of the market place works to silence you as a Black or Native writer, so that what you have to say never reaches your audience, then your freedom and power as a writer is, in fact, thwarted. The writer is imprisoned— albeit metaphorically. The Canadian composition of this 54th Congress is a telling example of the silencing of the writer of colour. These writers who live and work and struggle in Canada have been made invisible by this conference. Not only is the representation of African, Asian and Native Canadian writers or moderators appallingly and unacceptably low, but the corralling of the majority of the visible Canadian writers into Next Generation events is a form of cultural apartheid. In this respect PEN Canada has replicated the First World/Third World or North/South polarity. We deplore this fact; we deplore the fact that this conference was funded by various levels of government whose policies specifically espouse, and at times even attempt to foster a multicultural, multi-racial and multi-ethnic society. The 54th PEN Congress is a travesty of these policies; it makes a mockery of any commitment to eradicate racism or classism in this society.

RECOMMENDATIONS

We urge delegates to keep these facts about Canada in mind as they debate the plight of writers in other countries. While it is important to consider the case of writers who are physically imprisoned, it is also important to think of

writers of colour in Western democracies such as Canada, who often face
racism in their daily and writing lives. These writers often live a "Third
World" reality in the affluent Western democracies. There is often, in fact,
a direct link between the power structure that supports the privileged
position of white writers in countries like Canada, the circumstances of
their own writers of colour, and the existence of regimes which imprison
writers in other countries.

Since the issues raised above relate directly to your commitment as PEN
members to "oppose any forms of suppression of freedom of expression,"
we urge you to raise these issues whenever you can at your panels and
readings.

Vision 21— Canadian Culture in the 21st Century
Multicultural Women Writers of Canada

Vision 21: Canadian Culture in the Twenty-first Century is a multi-racial,
multi-ethnic group of artists (formed in July, 1989), working in different
disciplines; their commitment is to eradicating racism, sexism, and
economic inequities from Canadian culture.

END NOTES:

1. Unfortunately, many other African Canadian writers and artists who had
been invited to distribute leaflets with us were unable to participate.
2. In 1990, M. Nourbese Philip lodged a complaint with the Ontario Press
Council against the *Globe and Mail* for the inaccuracies contained in the
article. The Council held for M. Nourbese Philip, that the *Globe and Mail*
had erred in its presentation of the facts.
3. Two names suggested that the writers were neither Anglo- nor Franco-
Canadian; we were, however, unsure of the race of the writers.

Am I a Nigger?
Incident at Congress

The Globe and Mail:

Am I a nigger because I exercised my democratic right to express my opinion outside Roy Thomson Hall on September 25? Am I a nigger because I dared to challenge the organizers of PEN Canada on the representation of writers of colour? Am I a nigger because I merely handed June Callwood a leaflet explaining our position? Or, am I a nigger because Ms. Callwood told me to "fuck off" ("Charges of Racism Spark Protest at Writers' Congress"— Sept. 26)?

On September 26, 1989, an early morning telephone caller with a male voice called me a nigger— my six-year-old daughter was on the extension. On September 26, 1989, the *Globe and Mail* carried fairly extensive coverage of a small demonstration I took part in, challenging the under-representation of Canadian writers of colour at the 54th PEN Congress. This article also described an incident involving the incoming president of PEN Canada, Ms. Callwood, myself, and other members of our group, Vision 21.

While I cannot and do not hold Ms. Callwood responsible for this phone call, I wish to point out that when someone of the stature of Ms. Callwood contemptuously dismisses allegations of racism in the manner she did, as well as being verbally abusive to a Black woman, such behaviour gives licence for individuals such as that early morning telephone caller to do what he did. By its frivolous treatment of the subject, replete with euphemisms, the *Globe*'s treatment of this incident in its editorial "PEN Pals" (Sept. 27) compounds this problem. It suggests that Ms. Callwood was tormented, and that lack of information on the part of the protesters was sufficient to provoke and, therefore excuse, her response. This may be what the media pundits call spin control, but to my mind it is irresponsible journalism. Ms. Callwood's response to us, combined with the *Globe*'s editorializing, is tantamount to declaring open season on individuals like myself.

I strongly object to the *Globe and Mail* calling me a tormentor. I merely approached Ms. Callwood and handed her a leaflet; we now know her response. Some guests supported our presence; others were displeased with us; still others engaged in debate with us, challenging us to prove what we claimed. Such is the nature of democracy. Ms. Callwood was the only one who became verbally abusive. Surely, if she had information that revealed our lack of information, in her role as incoming president of PEN, she ought to have challenged us with this information and not abused us. This sort of irrational response to legitimate protest comes close to being the verbal equivalent of actions of governments such as the Chinese government toward its dissenters.

I respect the invaluable work Ms. Callwood has done on behalf of the underprivileged in this country. Her election as president of PEN Canada was seen as a welcome development. All the more reason why her response to me and the other protesters outside Roy Thomson Hall on the evening of September 25, was appalling and ought not to be excused. Ms. Callwood ought, in fact, to take responsibility for her actions. I once again call upon her to apologize. Such an apology would go a long way toward clearing the path for a more enlightened debate on racism in writing and publishing in Canada. It might also dissuade callers hell-bent on persuading me that I am a nigger.

M. Nourbese Philip

The 6% Solution

EN-VISION, IF YOU CAN, an international conference of writers, hosted by Canada and held in Toronto. Fifty per cent of the Canadian delegates are Canadians of African, Asian or Native backgrounds presenting ideas and work that are contestory of the dominant Eurocentric culture. Would this be a Canadian conference? Certainly not, if one believes that "Canadian" means a dominant white group surrounded by micro-cultures, some of which are coloured brown, black or yellow. It is, if you see a Canada intent on righting, as much as any country can, the gross inequities and injustices which result from racism.

In a press release published in the *Toronto Star* (December 27, 1989), PEN Canada stated that African, Asian and Native peoples comprise six per cent of the Canadian population. By cleverly manipulating the base figure, but not the actual numbers, PEN Canada showed that the representation of Canadians from these backgrounds at the 54th International PEN Congress held last fall, varied from 12 to 23 per cent. Percentages changed, but the actual number of African, Asian and Native delegates to the Congress remained constant at seven.

In the Canadian context, however, six per cent represents poor schooling, high infant mortality rates, under or unemployment, premature deaths, coerced sterilization, police harassment and poor housing. Six per cent of Canada's population faces these problems and more for the simple reason that their skins are black or brown. The high incidence of these pathological social conditions within this six per cent of the Canadian population is disproportionate to the numerical presence of Africans, Asians and Natives in Canadian society.

Six per cent is also replete with the historical resonances of racism: the genocidal effect of European settlement on Native peoples; the building of this country by Asian labourers who were then relegated to second class status; the internment of Canadians of Japanese heritage during World War II; the discrimination against Africans, including Black Empire Loyalists who fled to Canada— after being promised land— only to confront racism once they got here; the externally induced immigration to Canada of many African Caribbean people who followed the capital taken out of the Caribbean by Canadian banks; a racist immigration policy which, because of a need for cheap and unskilled labour, has only recently begun to let in darker-skinned people, and which still discriminates against them by the positioning and numbers of immigration offices around the world. In Canada, six per cent constitutes what is left *after* imperialism, capitalism and colonialism have done their dirty business, and then suggest that business ought to be as usual. Six per cent, in fact, represents the survivors.

All of this is not to dismiss the need, at times, for formulae designed to achieve equity and parity between those of the dominant culture and those who have traditionally faced discrimination. We ought not, however, to forget that this is essentially what they are— arbitrary formulae for trying to redress ancient and not-so-ancient injustices, to arrive at some sort of equity. If the formulae obscure what the source of the need for redress is, chances are that the system will remain intact and racism will continue to flourish.

How one uses percentages is integrally tied up with how one understands and interprets them. If one sees six per cent as merely another figure in the game of multiculturalism and forgets that, in the mathematics of racism in Canada, genocide *plus* racism leave a remainder of six per cent, then as a figure six per cent can be infinitely manipulated to prove anything. If the goal is merely to reflect the various percentages in the population, then the manipulation that PEN Canada engaged in, while being extreme, is to be expected; more than that, PEN Canada is, therefore, correct in its conclusions that it over-represented in percentage terms (though not to the degree that they suggest), the presence of Africans, Asians and Natives in Canada. If, however, the goal is to redress, through every means possible, a long and destructive legacy of oppression, racism and exploitation in this country, then those who cleverly manipulate figures while leaving the essential structure intact, do nothing but perpetuate this particular system.

Vision 21 starts from the position that sees culture as an integral and vital aspect of *how* a system reproduces and reaffirms itself. If, therefore, the system in question, in this case Canadian society, is racist in its well-springs, then it follows that the official and dominant culture of that society and its articulation will reflect that racism, even in such a supposedly esoteric practice as writing. What the South African writer, J.M. Coetzee, accurately describes as the "ideological superstructure of publishing, reviewing and criticism" plays a vital role here in Canada in the shoring up of racist traditions.

Vision 21 desires to make changes in the arts in Canada, not to assert power over anyone, as has been suggested; not to prove that Chinese or African culture, for instance, is necessarily better than English culture, but to create an equal respect for each. Vision 21, therefore, ends up in a very different place from those who limit themselves to looking at percentages and conclude that because they have "over-represented" those percentages, God must be in his heaven and all's well with the world.

To eradicate racism in Canada and to establish it as an anti-racist society, Canada needs what Martin Luther King, pacifist though he was, called a "revolution of values and a radical relocating of power." Nothing less will suffice. Those individuals and groups interested in working toward this goal must begin with an understanding that racism is often not the result of an individual act, but a consequence of rules, procedures and criteria that all together have a discriminatory effect, *regardless* of motive or intent.

If we are to begin to make relevant and meaningful changes, merely looking at percentages will not suffice. What follows are some of the issues which must galvanize us all into intelligent debate:

— how must the white dominant culture and groups which hold power change so that power devolves to other groups which have traditionally been excluded?;
— how to prevent continued ghettoization and containment of African, Asian and Native cultures by the dominant culture;
— are the new and emergent voices from African, Asian and Native cultures powerful enough to challenge the dominant culture?;
— is Canadian culture to be formed by taking the best from Native, African, Asian and other immigrant cultures, along with English and French culture to create a new entity?;
— what constitutes appropriation of other cultures, such as Native culture, by the dominant culture?;

— how to make the "ideological superstructure of publishing,
reviewing and criticism" more responsive to, and respectful of,
writers from other cultures, as well as more responsible for the
public monies it receives;
— how to open a space for emerging voices which are profoundly
contestory of the dominant culture.

Whatever the discipline, the work of the artist and writer
consists in giving tangible form to their imagined ideal. The
possibility of accomplishing this is, however, closely linked to
the material conditions which are, in turn, very much affected
by racism, sexism and economic inequality. If artists and writers
are truly interested in creating conditions minimally affected by
these problems, we must eschew the sort of clever manipulation
of statistics described above. Only by so doing can we begin to
debate and discuss how best to go about making real those
imagined ideals.

END NOTES:

Brenda Lem (artist and filmmaker) and Gillian Morton, both members of
Vision 21, contributed their ideas and thoughts and time to the issues
discussed above.

M. Nourbese Philip originally submitted this piece to the *Toronto Star* in an
attempt to counter the spurious arguments that PEN Canada made
concerning statistics (*Toronto Star*, December 27, 1989) and the
representation of African, Asian and Native voices. *The Star* held on to the
piece for several weeks and when Philip contacted them about its
publication, she was told that the PEN issues had become stale news. The
Toronto Star never published the article.

Publish + Be Damned

MINORITY— READ ASIAN, AFRICAN AND NATIVE— writers have difficulty getting their books published because there is too small an audience and market for such writers. Being essentially business people, publishers are, therefore, unwilling to publish such work. This is the substance of the argument making the rounds in literary circles— from panel discussions at the 54th PEN Congress, held last fall in Toronto, and the letters page of *NOW Magazine*, to the "Notes from the Inner Circle" of *Books in Canada*. The underlying factors in this argument, however, have less to do with audience and market forces and more to do with racism.

Implicit in the argument outlined above is the assumption that the publishing industry in Canada is market driven. It is not. Apart from foreign-controlled houses, the Canadian publishing industry is heavily subsidized by various levels of government— either through arts council assistance or through the direct transfer of funds. In 1989, subsidies from the federal government through the Canada Council and direct transfers, amounted to some $15 million; on the provincial level in Ontario, there was $2.5 million in guaranteed loans and interest payments, and just under $1 million in arts council assistance. Market forces do not determine the publishing activity of those publishing houses receiving subsidies; if they did, these houses would not be in business.

The argument also assumes that if you are a Canadian writer of Native, Asian or African background, the only possible audience for your work is one comprised of individuals of the same ethnic background; this is erroneous, narrow-minded, and even racist. While writers like James Baldwin, Salman Rushdie, Toni Morrison, Alice Walker, Joy Kogawa and Austin Clarke may have written their works with audiences from their own particular cultures in mind, their success beyond those cultures clearly belies the argument that writers are limited to audiences of their particular ethnic or racial group, and that, therefore, their work can only be marketed within that group.

One frequent explanation for the success of such writers is merit: that because the books written by these writers are good books, everyone (and if we are honest, we must admit that "everyone," in this context, means the white mainstream audience) can read them. However, these books become, by definition, "good" books *because* the white mainstream audience reads them. The argument, refined, would go something like this: Canadian writers of African, Asian or Native backgrounds have a difficult time getting their work published because of the small size of their respective ethnic audiences, except if their works are "good" enough to appeal to a white audience.

While quality is an important consideration in the publication of any work (and the talents of the writers mentioned above go a long way in explaining their success), as important is what the South African writer, J.M. Coetzee, describes as "that vast and wholly ideological superstructure of publishing, reviewing and criticism" which together all work to market books within the dominant culture.

Works by writers from cultures other than the dominant one often succeed in the publishing world of this culture, not only

because they may be well-written, but also because they satisfy
certain ideas already in existence in the dominant culture.
Authors like V.S. Naipaul and his nephew Neil Bissoondath are
both examples of writers who catapulted to fame on the savage
and, at times, racist critique of the "Third World." In the former
case the talent is indisputable; in the latter, *debatable*. Alice
Walker's mega-success and position as Queen of Black womanist
writing in the United States is, in no small way, based on her
work *The Colour Purple*, tapping into certain deep-seated traditions in America. Celie and Shug eventually become small
entrepreneurs, pulling themselves up by their own efforts. Not
to mention the theme of lesbianism, which is much more
acceptable within the white feminist movement than in African
American communities. In comparison, Toni Morrison's *Song
of Solomon* is a far more profound and accomplished work; it is
also far more seriously contestory of the dominant, white racist
culture of America. Until very recently, Morrison had never won
a major literary prize in the United States, a fact which generated
a letter of support by fellow African American writers (*New York
Review of Books*, 1988) for her contribution to African American
letters.

One unfortunate result of the workings of the "ideological
superstructure" is the one-only syndrome— at any one point in
time there can only be *one* great African American writer, while
many other equally talented writers languish in relative obscurity.
It appears that the price of admission for one or two is the
exclusion of all other writers from the group.

Publishing, reviewing and criticism are by no means unbi-
ased activities; individuals who work in these areas reflect and
represent certain political and social attitudes, which in turn
affect which work will not only get published— this is often the

easiest part of "publication"— but also reviewed and criticized. This does not mean that an evaluation of a book is a purely political and ideological act, bearing no relevance to its quality, nor does it mean that a work by an African Canadian author which is rejected by publishers is necessarily bad. Doris Lessing's "experiments" with her Jane Somers novels, which saw her own publishers rejecting work by her under a different name, should put an end to such assumptions. It does, however, mean that an important part of the assessment of value and quality of a work is a judgement that is all of a piece with wider political, cultural and social values.

In a recent piece that appeared in *Books in Canada*, Governor General's Award winner Erin Mouré writes that the belief that the only possible audience for a Black writer is a Black audience, "covers up and renders silent the influence (when they're allowed to be heard) minority writers have within our culture(s) on the experience and perceptions of all (including white) writers." What appears indisputable, however, is that the only audience that matters in Canada *is* the white audience, and how members of the "ideological superstructure"— reviewers, critics and publishers alike— interpret the interests and needs of that audience. Clearly, this superstructure sees the Canadian audience as narrow-minded, provincial and unable to read and enjoy anything but work written *by* white writers, with the odd dash of ethnic literary spice proffered by one or two carefully chosen writers.

What is, however, more disturbing about the arguments suggesting that certain writers write only for their specific ethnic and/or racial audience, is that the proponents of these arguments are often the very ones who argue for the untrammelled nature of the writer's imagination, and his or her right to enter any culture or society imaginatively— in particular minority cultures such as those of Native Canadians— and write about it. But for which audience? The white or Native audience? Pushing the argument to its logical conclusion, it would proceed as follows: a white writer may use any aspect of any culture— in this instance, African, Asian or Native— in his or her writing because the imagination is free. Such a writer can write about those things for white audiences. When writers from those very groups write about their cultures, it can only be for their own particular cultural or racial audiences. Because these audiences are so small, the likelihood of a writer from one of these "minority cultures" getting his or her work published is, understandably, limited. Whites will, however, read such material, *provided it is written by one of their own.*

There exists, however, a historical example which damns this narrow-minded approach even further: the spread of English literature throughout the Empire and, more recently, the Commonwealth. Without an inkling of English life, black and brown subjects of the British Empire were expected to ingest its literature, unmediated by any lived experience of the culture. The entire livelihood and future of these subjects often depended on understanding daffodils, nightingales, fogs and winter, while living with constant sunshine, hummingbirds and poinsettias. Yet these people successfully grasped many, if not all, of the nuances of English literature. That experience could be described as one of the most successful examples of readers reading across boundaries— albeit in one direction and as a direct consequence of imperial power. As an approach to the study of literature, the imperial model is not to be recommended; we must, however, question whether Canadian readers are unable to do what readers with considerably fewer material resources have been doing for the last several decades. Or is it that publishers and reviewers aren't giving them half the chance?

Reading is an essentially profoundly anarchic act, particularly if readers have access to work that challenges hackneyed and stereotypical ideas and patterns of thought. Traditionally, white Canadians have not only read works about their own cultures. English literature is, in fact, replete with subject matter and characters taken from other cultures and races— *written by white authors*. What is new is that writers *from* these cultures— African, Asian and Native— that have been written *about*, are now coming to voice. However, the wholly ideological superstructure of publishing, reviewing and criticism in Canada has failed to take up the challenge that the presence of other voices in Canada offers.

The reason why African, Asian and Native writers have difficulty getting published has little to do with the audience and markets and much to do with racism and power: power to exercise that racism by deciding which books ought and ought not to be published, reviewed and critiqued. Fear is the other important variable at work here: fear, as James Baldwin wrote, on the part of those who hold power at "being described by those they've been describing for so long."

It was also Baldwin's opinion that the inevitable result of Black voices being heard was that the concept of colour would become obsolete. A large part of the current debate over the writer and voice has to do with certain voices— certain *Canadian* voices— not being heard. Publishers, particularly those who have the luxury— albeit a dubious one— of not being driven by market forces, can play an invaluable role in beginning to treat all Canadian writers equally.

If publishers in the dominant culture who get the lion's share of these disbursements, insufficient as they are, will not voluntarily make the changes needed to ensure that their lists represent good writing from all sectors of Canadian society, there ought to be a concerted effort to pressure the various levels of government to establish mechanisms to ensure greater responsibility. Publishers receiving government monies could be made to report on affirmative action policies in their businesses: for instance, the number of manuscripts from African, Asian and Native Canadians they have seriously considered over the last fiscal year.

Sweeteners could also be added to the funding pot so that those publishers who have shown a commitment to publishing work by writers from the communities mentioned above would be encouraged and rewarded by larger grants. This would mean that publishers would actively have to seek out such work and would necessarily have to have readers who were sensitive to the material.

Having such readers would also mean that even the definition of terms such as "good" literature would begin to change. We ought then to see a more comprehensive definition of quality, and not one that is predominantly European.

I am not advocating the production of literature by quota, where a publisher would be required to publish a certain number of works by writers of certain ethnic backgrounds. I am, however, calling for an innovative use of funding which will have the desired effect of making publishers look seriously at work by African, Asian, and Native Canadians, and, in many instances, for the first time.

While such changes undoubtedly make for more bureaucratic work for publishers, they will only become necessary if publishers fail to take up the challenge of their multi-ethnic and multi-racial audiences and writers.

The arts councils and other funding agencies must also be made more responsive and responsible to African, Asian and Native Canadian publishers and writers and their particular problems. Their staff as well as their juries ought to reflect the presence of Canadians of African, Asian and Native backgrounds. There ought also to be a concerted effort made to educate staff, jury and board members to the validity of other cultures.

There is a notorious precedent in Canada for this deliberate and conscious tinkering with the "vast superstructure of publishing, reviewing and criticism." CanLit was, in fact, created by government fiat. It has succeeded in producing many fine writers who have achieved renown domestically *and* internationally.

There is undoubtedly a challenge to marketing books in cultures that are strongly and traditionally oral. The challenge only becomes an impediment if the will is lacking. As has been noted in the marketing of books by Black writers in the United States, one good review by a preacher is worth ten *New York Times* book reviews. In taking up the challenges around publishing books by African, Asian and Native writers, Canadian publishers could, in the nineties, give new meaning to the expression "publish and be damned," and in so doing open the *Can* in Canlit to allow all the other voices that make up Canada to be heard.

The New Jerusalem

In two and a half minutes

In the last three months, no less than three organizations comprised of African Canadian artists and other artists of colour— the Black Film and Video Network, Full Screen, and the Canadian Artists Network, Black Artists in Action (CAN-BAIA)— have received funding from various arts funders; the 1990 *Festival of Festivals*, for the first time in its history, hired three persons of colour, among whom was an African Canadian programmer of Canadian film. Nineteen-ninety also saw the following changes: the Canada Council struck the Committee for Racial Equality in the Arts to look at its funding practices as they relate to racial and ethnic "minorities"; the Toronto Arts Council hired an African First Nations Canadian as consultant to look at its funding practices and how they relate to issues of cultural and racial sensitivity; the National Gallery in Ottawa retained the services of an African Canadian curator to program a Black British film series; for the first time in its history, a Black nominee was short-listed for the Governor General's awards; arts councils actively solicited African Canadians and other persons of colour to sit on their awards panels; and more African, Asian, and Native writers have appeared on

TVOntario's *Imprint* show than ever before. No panel discussion is now complete without its token person of African, Asian, or Native heritage, albeit the topic may continue to be handled in the standard Eurocentric way. Has the "New Jerusalem" arrived in Ontario along with the NDP— at least in matters related to arts, culture, and race? Or is it merely the old Babylon in partial blackface?

This remarkable flurry of activity by arts organizations and groups to make racially-sensitive changes— in many instances these changes represent at least a 100% increase— suggests that the systems are changing and responding to criticisms of their Eurocentric and, therefore, racist biases. We must, however, question whether these changes are fundamental and lasting, or whether the systems are merely changing so as to remain the same. By their very nature, organizations function so as to perpetuate themselves *as they are*; this, combined with systemic racism, suggests that the system is merely fine-tuning its racism and becoming more sophisticated in how it continues to remain the same. It will, therefore, become even more difficult to identify, challenge, and eradicate racism.

The first wave of anti-racist work in the arts and culture in Toronto began some ten years ago with piecemeal challenges by individuals and groups such as De Dub Poets, who confronted dominant Eurocentric organizations like the League of Canadian Poets over the latter's racism. The issues around racism, writing and publishing that surfaced around the break-up of The Women's Press in 1988 moved the debate forward a painful quantum leap. This period culminated in the fall of 1989 with the public confrontation between PEN Canada and Vision 21 over the poor representation of African, Asian, and Native writers at the 1989 PEN conference in Toronto. This confrontation— a watershed event— and its repercussions mark the end of the first period of anti-racist work in the arts and culture in Toronto.

The significance of this event lay in the fact that PEN was seen very much as a "progressive" organization; if such an organization was being publicly shown up as manifesting all the shortcomings and neglect that systemic racism generates, how much more must other organizations be falling short? So, for instance, although the call for submissions to the recently published anthology *Language in Her Eye* had by that time been closed for some time, immediately after the PEN/Vision 21 confrontation, the editors issued another call for submissions, this time to many more African, Asian, and Native writers.

The run-off from this watershed event is, in no small way, directly responsible for the various changes mentioned in the first paragraph. These changes have now seguéd into what I call the second phase of anti-racist work. The following case is illustrative of how an organization, while *appearing* to make changes in the area of race relations, is able to maintain a bulwark against opinion that is critical of the dominant culture in the area of racism.

Over the past year, the print and electronic media have time and again found reasons to explain and justify why they could allow full expression to the views and opinions of a group such as PEN Canada, and why they could not do the same for Vision 21. And never once did they use the word censorship. To these reasons we must now add the requirement of "good television."
— Letter dated September, 1990, to TVO from Vision 21

On October 9, 1989, the subject matter of TVO's *Imprint*

show, hosted by Jennifer Gibson and Paul Roberts, was the 1989 PEN conference; spokespersons for the latter event were June Callwood and Graeme Gibson. During the course of the show, the hosts and guests discussed the leafletting of the PEN Gala by Vision 21. Vision 21 considered comments made about those involved in the leafletting to be derogatory of the issues around racism and anti-racism, as well as of the participants. During this show analogies were drawn, for instance, between Vision 21 and witch hunters. Vision 21 launched a complaint to the CRTC on the grounds that TVO, in its failure to give Vision 21 a voice to present its side of the issue, was in breach of its mandate to represent Ontarians and their views in an equitable and non-racist way. During the course of the complaint procedure and several weeks *after* the CRTC had sent details of Vision 21's complaint to it, TVO's chairman, Bernard Ostry, guaranteed in writing to the CRTC that Vision 21 would have a forum on its 1990-91 *Imprint* season.

In the same letter Mr. Ostry dismissed Vision 21's complaints about TVO's systemic racism as "egregious and totally unfounded" and as an example of TVO meeting the cultural needs of Ontario's minorities he referred to the then very recent hiring of Toronto dub poet, Clifton Joseph, as the third story editor on the *Imprint* show. To my mind there is a strong and causal connection between Vision 21's complaint to the CRTC and the hiring of the only non-white story editor on the *Imprint* series.

Vision 21 accepted TVO's offer, assuming that the forum which the latter offered would be similar to the one provided to PEN Canada, and would allow Vision 21 to talk about its work and issues around racism and culture. The requirements of "good TV" were, however, to provide an impossible bar to

Vision 21 being given such a forum.

TVO first attempted to invite this writer as a guest to discuss her own work and to debate with another guest. Vision 21's response was that TVO's offer ought to be to the *organization* and not to an individual; Vision 21 felt that it was entitled, at least, to a format similar to that provided PEN Canada— two guests in discussion with the host on issues relevant to its work. TVO's response, through *Imprint*'s present host, Daniel Richler, was that straight-on interviews did not make for "good TV," and that Vision 21 could "win more people to its side" by engaging in a debate. (In case you didn't know it, folks, all those straight-on interviews that make up the backbone of television talk shows make for bad TV!)

Vision 21 then queried whether TVO's offer of a forum was dependent on the former engaging in a debate. In response, TVO presented Vision 21 with the unbeatable offer of the year— *two and a half minutes of straight-on interview time*. (Andy Warhol, get back!) The alternative? Participate in a debate format. And how did TVO get to that figure? Two and a half minutes represents "the portion of the Gibson/Callwood interview to which Vision 21 took exception" (October 12, 1990, letter from TVO to Vision 21). Vision 21 reopened the complaint to the CRTC on the grounds that the initial offer by TVO was not *bona fide*.[1]

The irony of this situation is that Vision 21 found the presence of a non-white story editor at *Imprint* to be singularly unhelpful, despite the fact that the position was created *as a direct result* of the former's complaint to the CRTC. The position clearly carried no power and, in fact, during "negotiations" between Vision 21 and TVO, Mr. Joseph admitted to this writer, albeit somewhat ironically, that his function was merely "to carry messages" in the discussions between Mr. Richler and Vision 21.

Little did TVO know, however, that in offering Vision 21 two and a half minutes of television time, it was striking the signature note for phase two of anti-racist work in the arts and culture in Ontario and possibly, Canada. Many of the changes outlined in the first paragraph are, in fact, the equivalent of the two and a half minutes of television time TVO offered Vision 21, and will remain just that unless arts and cultural organizations are pushed to give African Canadians and other persons of colour equal time. Equal time in this context means making significant structural, and not cosmetic, changes.

Two of the most significant impediments to making these changes remain co-optation and collaboration. These are harsh words that dog all struggles. In South Africa, a harsh and retributive justice resulted in collaborators being necklaced in public. In Canada we repudiate such harsh measures believing our situation to be, after all, very different. But what does one do when the struggle to bring real change is compromised? What does one do when individuals acquire expertise working in community groups, for instance, which often springboard them into plum government jobs, where these same individuals, by refusing funding, then put the boot to those very organizations that trained them? What does one do when individuals publicly and harshly criticize organizations of the dominant culture for their racism, and at the first opportunity rush to join those very structures, becoming all of a piece with the very mandarins they once criticized? What does one do when the system is only too willing to use these individuals in its overwhelming need to survive unchanged? And in the face of blandishments and seducements as happened recently when the chairman of TVO,

Mr. Bernard Ostry, invited this writer to dine with him at the annual Writers' Development Trust dinner, what does one do? How does one avoid compromising one's self while challenging their two and a half minutes?

I do not for one minute suggest that critically-aware individuals ought not to work for, with, or have contacts with, organizations of the dominant culture. Such a position is foolhardy at best and suicidal at worst. To survive and feed themselves and their families, Africans in the New World have *always* had to work at jobs they did not like, or in situations that demeaned or compromised them. Crossing the border from the private space into the space of those who oppress you, is nothing new for groups such as these. The struggle for equity and dignity can and must take place on all fronts and in all arenas. But co-optation means that the struggle is either compromised or stops entirely, and collaboration that there is active work afoot to prevent the struggle from coming to fruition.

Those at the centre of systems of power believe and have always believed that those in opposition want in. The centre is, after all, about protecting "us" against "them." And those at the centre believe that those in opposition, because they want in, are all prepared to sell their birthright for the traditional mess of pottage. And because others have done this, it makes this possibility all the more real. Many individuals, however, *do* choose to work from a position outside the centre— from the margins. (I use margin in the sense of it being a frontier.) And any truly democratic society, of which I know none, needs the frontier of the margin as much as, if not more than, the centre. Without the margin, the centre remains smug and unchallenged— a breeding ground for abuses against the individuals and groups perceived as unimportant.

How *do* we avoid compromising ourselves? How do we help others in their efforts not to compromise themselves? And how do we challenge those organizations that are only content to offer us two and a half minutes— in whatever guise? The only way out of this is to have as clear an understanding as possible as to why we're objecting to, or challenging, the dominant culture.

Is it *only* so that we too may enter and have our share of the American dream or the Canadian nightmare— two cars and a colour TV set complete with *Imprint*? Or is it so that we can change the system so fundamentally that *any* who so desire may enter, regardless of race, colour, creed, or class? Isn't it because those of us who had our souls fired in the maelstrom of racial abuse and exploitation in the New World, understand the rapaciousness of a system based on the twin pillars of racism and capitalism, the latter now embraced as the panacea for the world's ills rather than their progenitor? And isn't it because we want to change that and not to help the system change so that it can remain the same?

In its effort to survive unchanged, the system will *always* ensure that the numbers of people of colour remain small and never attain that critical mass often necessary for change rather than reform. In fact, this country's immigration laws and policies are designed to work so that Africans, Asians, and other peoples of colour will *always* remain a token presence in Canada. The premise behind this approach— the six per cent solution as I have dubbed it elsewhere in this work[2]— is that, since such people represent a very small portion of the population, it is enough if their representation in organizations and groups merely and barely reflects their percentage presence in the society. Such arguments, while being fundamentally flawed, have limited relevance to city states which Toronto and other large urban centres have become, where people of colour often represent substantial percentages of the population.

Two and a half minutes do not a revolution make, and individuals and groups involved in anti-racist work in the arts now have to develop strategies to increase the yield of those two and a half minutes. Those choosing to work on the frontiers of the margins of arts and culture communities must continue to be critical of organizations which, in the present climate of anti-racist fashionableness, merely make cosmetic changes while leaving the underlying structures intact.

One Black employee, consultant, worker, or panel member cannot make fundamental changes to an organization, and it is unfair to expect them to do so; it is not unfair, however, to expect them to help to put hairline fractures in these organizations. Often the hairline fracture is all we can do, while hoping that down the road somewhere, with enough such fractures, the structures will collapse.

African Canadians do have a right to question those individuals who have got into positions of prestige and power on the coat-tails of the struggles of others. And even if the link is not that direct, individuals and groups do have a right to question what persons from their own racial or ethnic groups are doing, to help make meaningful structural changes in their places of employment. Individuals who understand the nature of systemic racism and how organizations, by using strategies of co-optation and collaboration, adjust to survive, *can* help to make the work of those on the frontiers of the margins easier. One well-placed, well-intentioned, and critically-thinking Black individual in an organization is worth several who have been co-opted.

What follows are checklists which may be useful in assisting us all in this second period of the anti-racist struggle in Babylon.

The questions should be used to clarify the issues. Individuals and groups are urged to develop questions that pertain specifically to the organizations in which they work. The questions can be used as a monitoring device of one's self, others, and organizations. They could also be useful in collecting data on organizations; such information is indispensable in challenging the claims of organizations that they are making structural changes. We cannot isolate ourselves from the dominant culture and we will all, at one time or another, be called on to work within its systems. We cannot, however, afford to be complacent if we are serious about replacing Babylon with the New Jerusalem.

TWO AND A HALF MINUTE CHECKLISTS

These checklists are by no means exhaustive and can be expanded, shortened, and adjusted to suit your own needs and situation.

ORGANIZATIONS

1. Is the person the only one hired from his/her racial group?
2. How much power do they have in the organization?
3. Has the organization only hired persons of colour at the margins of power?
4. Have they had to lose their cultural specificity and uniqueness to function in the organization?
5. How does the organization deal with other issues around race?
6. Does the staff of the organization remain predominantly white or does it reflect the multi-racial nature of society?

7. Is the organization only offering "two and a half minutes" in terms of change?

8. Are there any African, Asian, or Native Canadians in positions of power?

9. If there are any such individuals in power, how are they exercising their power? Are they gatekeeping or facilitating the entry of other persons of colour?

10. Do African, Asian, or Native Canadians have any political voice in the organization?

INDIVIDUALS

Questions to ask yourself

1. Am I the only one from my group hired?

2. How much power do I have in the organization?

3. Do I have to become "white" to survive in the organization?

4. How am I heard within the organization?

5. How am I being silenced within the organization?

6. Is my voice delegitimized? If so, how?

7. What am I encouraged to say within the organization?

8. What am I discouraged from saying within the organization?

9. Do I have any influence or power within the organization?

10. Do others from my group have influence or power within the organization?

11. Do I/they have a political voice in the organization?

12. What kind of contact can I have with other people of colour in the organization?

13. Does institutional hierarchy prevent me making contact with other people of colour?

14. How well do I consider myself to be representing the interests of

African Canadians/people of colour in my work?

15. Do I consider it a part of my job to be representing the interests of others from my group?

16. How much is expected of me from members of my racial group?

17. Do I consider this unreasonable?

18. Can I get more African Canadians/people of colour hired?

19. Where is my voice heard in the organization?

20. Do I have access to levels of power?

21. Have I been hired at the margins of power?

INDIVIDUALS

Questions to ask of other individuals

1. Does the individual remain in touch with others from his/her racial group?

2. What is the individual doing to represent the interests of African Canadians/people of colour in the organization?

3. What is the individual doing to make relevant changes within his/her organization?

4. Does the individual make an effort to explain what he/she is doing to represent the interests of African Canadians/people of colour?

5. What are your expectations of this individual?

6. Do you consider them reasonable?

7. Does he/she consider them reasonable?

8. Is this individual aware of expectations placed on him/her?

9. Is there a discrepancy between what the individual says and what he/she is doing?

10. Does the individual set off your bullshitometer?

11. How respectful is the individual to anti-racist work being done by others?

Thanks to Cameron Bailey for his assistance in preparing these checklists.

END NOTES:

1. Since the first publication of this piece in *FUSE*, the CRTC has turned down Vision 21's appeal of its decision not to proceed any further with the complaint against TVO.
2. See "The 6% Solution," elsewhere in this collection.

Why Multiculturalism Can't End Racism

A national culture is the whole body of efforts made by a people
in the sphere of thought to describe, justify and praise the action
through which that people has created itself and keeps itself in
existence.— *The Wretched of the Earth*, Franz Fanon

AT ITS MOST BASIC, MULTICULTURALISM describes a configuration
of power at the centre of which are the two cultures recognized
by the constitution of Canada— the French and the English—
and around which circumnavigate the lesser satellite cultures.
Native culture, to date, remains unrecognized by the Constitution.

The configuration of power appears to be designed to
equalize power among the individual satellite cultures, and
between the collectivity of those cultures and the two central
cultures, the French and English. The mechanism of multiculturalism is, therefore, based on a presumption of equality, a
presumption which is not necessarily borne out in reality.

Because it pretends to be what it is not— a mechanism to
equalize all cultures within Canada— it ought not to surprise us
that multiculturalism would be silent about issues of race and
colour.

The Ontario government in its official policy on multiculturalism, *Multiculturalism: A New Strategy for Ontario*, recognizes the special concerns that colour and race present, and addresses those concerns within their policy. The new federal bill, Bill C-18, soon to be the Department of Multiculturalism and Citizenship Act, does not even define multiculturalism, let alone mention race or colour.

A long historical overview of the formation of Canada reveals that this country was, as was the United States, shaped and fashioned by a belief system that put white Europeans at the top of society and Native and African people at the bottom. This ideology, for that is what it is, assigned more importance to European cultures and values than those of the Native or African.

The Canadian examples are numerous: its genocidal practices against Natives; its past and present treatment of the Black Empire Loyalists who fled to the Maritimes; the various immigration acts which record Canada's preference for white Europeans; Canada's past treatment of Chinese and Indian immigrants; its refusal to allow entry to large numbers of Africans or Asians until very recently; Canada's treatment of its citizens of Japanese heritage in World War II; its present treatment of Asian refugees; and the present location and quantity of immigration offices around the world. To these must be added Canada's reluctance to allow Jews to seek refuge here during World War II.

These examples all constitute evidence of a nation founded upon a belief in white and European supremacy, of which racism, as we presently know it, is an offshoot. In his study of the right wing in Canada, *Is God a Racist?* Stanley R. Barrett writes that, "racism in Canada has been institutionalized... as deeply rooted as that in the United States," the difference being that Canada has always put a more polite face on its racism.

Wherever the European went, whether he was English,

French, German, Spanish, Dutch or Portuguese, he took with him this particular gospel— that the Native and indigenous peoples he encountered, who were also not white, were to be brutalized, enslaved, maimed, or killed and, where necessary, used to enrich him personally and/or his particular European country.

Wherever you find the European outside Europe, there you will find this particular pattern and method of settlement. The settlement of Canada was no exception to this rule.

The source of this belief— that the light pigmentation of one's skin bespeaks one's superiority and entitles one to destroy those of a darker hue, and/or unjustly enrich one's self at their expense— is a complex one and cannot be explored here. Suffice it to say that this belief system is, historically, an integral part of the cultural fabric of Canada. It is a belief system that is still with us today in many forms, and of which South Africa presents a telling and modern example.

Some might object to the use of the expression "white supremacy" on the grounds that it is an expression commonly used to describe extreme bigots who, along with other demands, openly advocate anti-Semitism, the repatriation of African and Asian immigrants, and a keep-Canada-white policy.

It is, however, an expression that accurately describes a certain historical and present-day reality as outlined above, and one which we must understand in order to grasp how thoroughly racism— the glue that holds the edifice of white supremacy together— permeates our societies.

What we have in Canada, therefore, are the manifestations of racial and ethnic prejudices between many of the so-called multicultural groups, because racism is not restricted only to relations between white and Black people. Depending on whether the variable of power is present, these prejudices may remain just that— prejudices— but prejudices which must be eradicated through a combination of education and legal remedies.

We also have, however, a larger and overarching structure posited on the ideology of white supremacy, one of the foundation stones of this country, and within which these other manifestations of racism function. To complicate matters even further, many of the white groups within the great multicultural pool come from cultures that have espoused these beliefs of white supremacy.

The net result is that Black people of African heritage will be found at the bottom of the multicultural pool. And below them will probably be found Natives.

What do we have when schools perfunctorily dump Black and Native students into dead-end, vocational programs; when police forces in our large urban centres treat their Asian and African communities as a sub-class to be policed differently and more harshly than white communities?

What do we have when justice systems and police forces treat Native people as a sub-class which receives a lesser form of justice than do white people; when statistics reveal that Black people are refused employment three times more frequently than whites?

What is it when publishers refuse to read manuscripts because they contain African Canadian characters, or when a museum under the guise of mounting an exhibition about African cultures, glorifies the imperial conquest of Africa?

What do we have? Racism or white supremacy? Does the difference in terminology really matter? And how, if at all, does multiculturalism affect these practices?

To the Indian, Jamaican or Micmac person on the receiving end of some of the practices described above, it often matters little what words you use to describe the actions that hurt and sometimes kill them. The results, whether we call it the ideology of white supremacy or racism, are the same— poor schooling, high unemployment, and inadequate housing to name but a few. All of which add up to the greatest tragedy of racism— wasted human potential and lives.

When you are black-skinned, it often matters little if the person refusing to rent to you is Polish-, Anglo- or Italian-Canadian. The result is the same. And multiculturalism, as we presently know it, has no answers to these or other problems such as the confrontations between the police forces in urban areas like Toronto and Montreal and the African Canadian communities that live there; it has no answers for the African Canadian or Native child shunted into a dead-end program in school.

In short, multiculturalism, as we know it, has no answers for the problems of racism, or white supremacy— unless it is combined with a clearly articulated policy of anti-racism, directed at rooting out the effects of racist and white supremacist thinking.

A society or nation such as Canada, founded on the principles of white supremacy and racism, cannot ever succeed in developing a society free of the injustices that spring from these systems of thought, without a clearly articulated policy on the *need* to eradicate these beliefs. And we cannot begin such an eradication by forgetting how one brutal aspect of Canadian culture was formed. It is for this reason that an understanding of the ideological lineage of this belief system is so important to any debate on racism and multiculturalism.

Despite its many critics, multiculturalism will not disappear.

Too many people benefit from it, and it is far too fancy a piece of window-dressing for a government to get rid of.

However, unless it is steeped in a clearly articulated policy of anti-racism, multiculturalism will, at best, merely continue as a mechanism whereby immigrants indulge their nostalgic love for their mother countries.

At worst, it will, as it sometimes does, unwittingly perpetuate racism by muddying waters between anti-racism and multiculturalism. It is not uncommon to read material from various government departments that use these words interchangeably so as to suggest that multiculturalism is synonymous with anti-racism. It is not. It never will be.

It is possible that Canadian society may come to accept that racism and white supremacist beliefs must no longer be a part of its culture. But only if there is a collective commitment to such a goal. It cannot do so merely by a policy of multiculturalism, which is a far less difficult task than eradicating those theories, beliefs and practices that rank humanity according to colour and race. Valuing people of all races and colour equally is a much wider, and infinitely more difficult, project than multiculturalism. Until this is accomplished, Canadians will not be able to derive the full benefits of multiculturalism— even in the limited sense in which this is ever possible.

Letter: June, 1991

James Baldwin

Dear James—

How did you survive it— did you, like me, find the woods cleansing of the pollution of racism— did you go for long walks exploring yourself as you did the paths? Maybe you sat exactly where I did in the woods, just before you crossed the planks over the brook— did you? Sit there and feel the specialness of creation— the gift that this world is and wonder just how it got so fucked up. And here I am in this country— the one that drove you out and away. I understand it so much better now and I've only been here two weeks plus two days— that's all it took to look the beast that's American racism in its face. How so, you might say— being with some of the best and finest any society can produce. True, but at what a cost— the still birth of all the dreams of the sixties and seventies. And don't get me wrong, but read me right— I am not talking about anyone being unkind, unpleasant, or even openly racist— quite, quite the contrary, but there *is* an apartheid in this country, all the more profound for the apparent freedom and lack of rules. Two realities— two solitudes to borrow a phrase from Canada's own political morass. My mind runs on you and on the work of one of your peers, Ralph Ellison's— *The Invisible Man.*

I am an invisible man... a man of substance, of flesh and bone, fibre
and liquids— and I might even be said to possess a mind. I am
invisible, understand, simply because people refuse to see me...
When they approach me they see only my surroundings,
themselves, or figments of their imagination— indeed, everything
and anything except me... That invisibility to which I refer occurs
because of a peculiar disposition of the eyes of those with whom I
come in contact. A matter of the construction of their inner eyes,
those eyes with which they look through their physical eyes upon
reality, I am not complaining, nor am I protesting either. It is
sometimes advantageous to be unseen, although it is most often
rather wearing on the nerves.

There is nothing more to say, is there— as often happens
with good writing— Ellison has said it all. And more. But let me
continue. I think of you, James, with your face remarkable in
any language, but your remarkable Black face, all angles and
lines, your wide wide mouth, and those eyes, those eyes that
seemed to register the worst and the best of what America is—
the cesspool and the heaven, both materialist. I think of you,
James, taking that face into town— were some eagerly friendly as
they are with me?— just a half beat too quick with their hello—
as if... *almost* as if they were both trying to prove that it didn't
matter you had a Black skin, *and* to subvert their own fear of you
you see reflected in their eyes, exactly and precisely as the camera
registers the image, albeit reversed, on its lens. But that's just it—
we are reversed, aren't we, in their sights. Did anyone offer to
take you swimming— or were the invitations such that you had
to say no? Did anyone ask what you were doing or writing and
show interest in it, or were you on the horns of a dilemma—
made too much of as a kind of aberrational one of a kind?

I walked through the woods today, James, the woods of New Hampshire, thinking of you, and there was and is a certain logic to my thinking of you beyond reading your quotation in the Colony newsletter: "The Colony has, for many years, lived in my mind as a refuge."

If Beale Street Could Talk, it would tell of the tears I shed for the woman in that book, whose name I now forget, and of the flame of recognition that came alight within me when I realized that literature could be peopled with those like myself— plain people, Black people, single women— yes, from this you could weave stories not just make news. I didn't have to be Russian like dear Anna, or English like Tess with a mouth I could never have, or American like Zelda, but she wasn't really a character, only Scott's wife. I could be Black and female and plain and have a life worth writing about, and now I would add worth writing. And isn't that what this sometimes gut-busting, tear-jerking, son-of-a-bitch art that we practise is all about— simply, yet profoundly and with great care, reflecting back to people their lives— their very own lives which they can then reclaim.

Dear James, I only saw you once— at the infamous Harbour-front Reading Series, but I thought of you today— here in New Hampshire— New England— Yankee country. Oh, James, so much and so very little, so very very little, has changed.

Nourbese

Excerpt from *South of the Border*
Previously unpublished

Immoral Fiction

A Casual Brutality
by Neil Bissoondath
Toronto: Macmillan of Canada, 1988

THE SIGNIFICANCE OF NEIL BISSOONDATH'S A *Casual Brutality* lies not in the work itself, but in the overwhelmingly positive and uncritical reception it has garnered here in Canada, and what that reception reveals about Canadian society. There is a very close relationship between the attitudes that engender this sort of reception for an extremely flawed work, and the historical and political forces that have produced a Neil Bissoondath. It is a relationship that has much to do with empire, colonialism and racism and it is these realities that Bissoondath goes to great lengths to evacuate from his novel. His work, A *Casual Brutality*, is in fact a brilliant example of social amnesia at work in a writer.

In a recent *Toronto Star* article (October 29, 1988), titled "The Solitude McLennan Didn't Anticipate," among the many things for which Bissoondath criticizes immigrants is their desire to gather together in groups or associations; like his character, Dr. Raj Ramsingh, he believes that the best and most effective way of "making it" in this society is to put as much distance between himself and those others— immigrants. Opinions and sentiments like these, expressed both by Bissoondath in his public pronouncements, and through his character, Raj, are those of the truly colonized mind, trained and schooled to despise all that has produced him except what the colonizer considers valuable. As in the case of his more famous uncle, V.S. Naipaul, writers like these, provided they have some ability, are guaranteed an immediate entré into the literary scene in whatever metropolis they happen to reside. They can express the racist sentiments of the colonizer without appearing to implicate the latter. Individuals such as Bissoondath feature significantly in the articulation of a more sophisticated brand of racism.

Despite the rapidity with which he wishes to shed his immigrant skin, and his obvious need to belong to Canadian society, A Casual Brutality is, ironically, the classic immigrant novel: Raj Ramsingh, a young Indian man, hates his country of birth, Casaquemada— a thinly disguised Trinidad, Bissoondath's country of origin— and comes to Canada in search of a better life. Why he hates his country we are never told, but hate it he does and quite rightly so. I say quite rightly so because nothing, according to Bissoondath, is loveable in Casaquemada, nothing is valuable; there is nothing that ought to be preserved or treasured. The people are shallow and greedy, the landscape threatens or is dirty, and there is only money and the lust for power. Naturally, therefore, fleeing the country is the only sensible thing anyone would do, fleeing it for one of the Northern metropolises, in this case, Toronto, where one can find all that is missing in the country of one's birth.

Where there was filth and dirt, there is now cleanliness, except for that eyesore, Kensington Market:

I had not come to Toronto to find Casaquemada, or to play the

role of ethnic, deracinated and costumed... this display of the
rakish, this attempt at Third World exoticism, seemed to me a
trap... The life implied by the Kensington Market gave me
nightmares for weeks to come...

Where people had been greedy and lusting for power in
Casaquemada, they were now kind: "it was remarkable how
people went out of their way to help." There are, however, other
immigrants who, heaven forbid, at times try to make eye contact
with him: "Only occasionally did distress arise: when the observer became observed, when Indians or Blacks sought me out
with their eyes, with nods of invitation." The one white racist
Raj meets is so clearly off balance we are able to dismiss him
easily— too easily; and with that dismissal the reader can turn
away from that most impolite of topics in Canadian society,
racism and, more particularly, institutional racism. Did Raj
Ramsingh come to Canada as a student or an immigrant? As
the former he would have had regular contact with the Immigration Department. Bissoondath has chosen to avoid those issues
which reveal the potential confrontation that always exists between immigrant and host society.

After he qualifies as a doctor, Raj, along with his wife and
young son return to Casaquemada, where money is in plentiful
supply on account of a massive increase in oil revenues. We find
out that like everyone else from Casaquemada, Raj was only
interested in making money— this was, in fact, the reason for his
return. The inevitable violence breaks out, the reasons for which
and the details of which are left vague. His wife and son are
murdered and he, having wisely taken out Canadian citizenship
as insurance before leaving for Casaquemada, returns to Canada— fade out to music and the picture of a plane taking the

grieving Raj Ramsingh back to his new homeland, Canada—
saviour to any immigrant who *will* find happiness, provided they
shed disturbing habits like trying to make eye contact with, and
setting up associations of fellow immigrants.

People come to Canada for a variety of reasons, some no
doubt, like Bissoondath, for the reasons he advances in his
novel, the same ones he has personally expressed. But surely
there is an obligation on a writer to do more with these facts.
The profound flaw at the heart of this novel is that it is structured
so as to lack any sort of tension. For the reasons stated above we
know that the protagonist will leave Casaquemada, the destina-
tion is irrelevant, provided it is not another Caribbean or "Third
World" country. The only question is why he returned to
Casaquemada in the first place. Without the tension set up by
competing loyalties, for instance, the work becomes a flat,
one-dimensional study in how to feed the hand that feeds you—
Canada in this case. And I must confess that reading this book
for review was one of the most tedious tasks I have ever engaged
in. Bissoondath ignores the exploration of powerful themes such
as exile and alienation to pander to the insatiable appetite of
North America for "Third World" violence.

The technical flaws in this work are many. The use of the
first person voice fails utterly: John Gardner, in *The Art of Fiction*,
writes that first person accounts usually work quite well when
the speech pattern of the character is one that comes out of a
culture that is highly oral, such as those of American Blacks, or
Jews, or Southerners; I would add Caribbean people to that list.
Bissoondath, however, has sacrificed the resource of a distinctive
speech pattern for a bland, formal type of standard English.
There is also more than a little self-indulgence in the work, which
at times appears to be autobiography masquerading as fiction,

or is it fiction masquerading as autobiography? All writers use autobiographical material as raw material for their work; I expect, however, that the writer's craft will transform this material in such a way that the reader either doesn't really care, or the question never arises. Not so in *A Casual Brutality*. Far too many incidents and characters appeared to have no real bearing on the story; I could only conclude that these incidents did take place, or that these characters did exist; the writer thought them interesting and so included them.

On many occasions, I was reminded of Gertrude Stein's comments on adjectives— that they "are not really and truly interesting. In a way anybody can know always has known that... because of course the first thing that anybody takes out of anybody's writing are the adjectives." "Anybody" clearly needed to go to work on *A Casual Brutality*. It is not enough, for instance, to have a "narrow, gravelled lane," but it must also be "hard-edged and filled with stone-studded ruts." Examples like this proliferate.

Like Naipaul, Bissoondath's attitude to women is at best ambivalent, at worst misogynist. Raj Ramsingh's wife is "pasty" and "slack faced," her breasts "pendulous." A female corpse which he and another medical student are dissecting *must* be Greek because all Greek women have big feet. The novel's most detailed description of a woman is a stripper plying her trade, crotch exposed to the world.

There is the usual healthy dose of racism: I had understood the expression "Chinaman" to be outdated and, because of its derogatory connotations, no longer used. Bissoondath, however, writes of a book illustrated with smiling Chinamen. He dismisses Hindu culture, as embodied by Raj's unenlightened grand-mother, as mere superstition. And in a long monologue by Raj's wife, he has her on three occasions within the same speech refer to a former friend from Latin America in a manner dismissive, if not contemptuous, of the area:

I once knew a girl from Latin America. From Venezuela or Colombia, some place like that. The kind of place that makes you think of drugs and oil and easy violence... Leda told me about her family in Panama or Mexico or wherever the hell she was from...

Still later on, she refers to Leda being from "Peru or Chile or wherever the hell she was from." Are we then to believe it inconsequential whether one is from Chile or Mexico, Central or South America?— each Latin American country being inter-changeable with another.

Bissoondath's treatment of landscape, though limited, is significant. Casaquemada had the "kind of vegetation, deceptive in its beauty, that could swallow you whole, a vision of green annihilation into which a man could disappear without a trace." It "festered with detritus," and "the air would suppurate with the caustic odours of vigorous decay." Canada and, more specifically, Toronto, presented "a rapid interplay of cloud, the rusting of the trees, the brittle crinkling of dried leaves," a maple leaf a "splinter of the beauty." This is, of course, all of a piece with a character who has no attachment to the land of his birth, from which he is completely alienated.

As Bissoondath himself writes, in his *Toronto Star* piece, referred to above, he was advised by a respected relative when he came to Toronto that:

Trinidad is behind you, and you have to forget Trinidad and Trinidad attitudes... Above all, look about you; look at the

landscape, try to enjoy it; try to understand the country and the
people and don't fall into the simple trap of thinking about race all
the time.

   Are we surprised that Casaquemada/Trinidad is presented
in very flat tones, lacking all perspective? Here there is no three
dimensionality of a country known, loved, and left— for whatever
reason. And for all his hatred of this place, Bissoondath writes
about it as a stranger, and not even a stranger with a perceptive
eye, for a stranger, I believe, would have made more attempt to
understand the workings of that society. He, and his character,
do not understand the place or, perhaps, what is even worse, in
light of the above exhortation to Bissoondath to understand
Canada, they do not care to understand it. That Raj hates
Casaquemada is clear; why he hates it we are never told. It is a
hatred which exists in a vacuum becoming, for that reason,
somewhat tedious.
   The distortions in this work are profound and amount to a
form of social amnesia. Russell Jacoby, in his work by the same
name, describes social amnesia as the process whereby the
ability, as well as the desire to remember atrophies. It is "the
forgetting and repression of the human and social activity that
makes and can remake society." Social amnesia serves to preserve
the status quo. What has been forgotten or unremembered is
the importation of the African and the Indian to the New World
to help fuel the British Empire; this is the backdrop to, and the
underlying generator of, both Raj Ramsingh's and Bissoondath's
social amnesia— it is this that distorts the novel.
   Bissoondath alludes to the Hindu idea of themselves as
racially superior. He makes no mention, however, of how the
two groups, Africans and Indians, were played off, one against

the other, by the then ruling British, thereby fuelling racial hostility on both sides, to which Raj and Bissoondath are both inheritors. He does not mention that, unlike the African, the Indian came with their religions, languages and cultures intact, and were allowed to keep them. He does not mention the fact that when the Indians came they met a country already cultivated and tamed by African labour, making it somewhat easier for them to become the lawyers and doctors he refers to in his work. In one of the most absurd examples of this mutilation of history and atrophying of memory, he places his character in an old fort where his thoughts turn to the British:

I thought grimly of the effort it must have taken the British [sic] to haul these pieces [of cannon] from the harbour, along what must have been, back then, at the beginning of the nineteenth century, little more than rutted roads up the steep, winding crumbling mountainside... I thought of the sweat and pain and the bitter cursing.

Is Bissoondath actually suggesting that in the nineteenth century white Englishmen were hauling *anything*, let alone cannons, *anywhere* in the British Empire where there were Blacks to do the work? Can he have forgotten that it would have been African, and possibly Indian, labour that would have been used? But he chooses *not* to remember that, for he writes later: "Those men had sweated and strained [he is here referring to white Englishmen!], had had other more valuable lessons to teach, but they paid only lip-service to their voiced ideals..."

Most of all, Bissoondath, because of his social amnesia, fails to see that the sad spectacle of his character as an individual filled with self-loathing, unable to attach himself anywhere, is very much a product of that experience of colonialism. For make no mistake, although Dr. Raj Ramsingh is headed towards his new home, Canada, and appears to love it, he will be unable to, seeing in it only what it can offer him, exactly as he returned to Casaquemada because of what *it* had to offer *him*. If Canada begins to slide into poverty, characters like Raj Ramsingh will just as easily pick themselves up and leave, seeking the next port to "love" and belong to.

On the issue of distortion: it *is* ironic and somewhat offensive that Bissoondath should use as the name of his fictional island, Casaquemada, a word which incorporates and plays on the name of that other fictional island, Quemada, the subject of the movie *Burn.* That film attempted a portrayal of Africans attempting to empower themselves by fighting for their freedom and asserting their rights and dignity as humans. Bissoondath's depiction of Casaquemada is a clumsy and brutal warping of that tradition— deliberate or otherwise.

There is a fundamental immorality at work in writers like Naipaul and Bissoondath. It is the immorality that manifests itself in a writer shitting on his country of birth, yet using the image of that country or place as Other in the psyches of Western and Northern countries, to fuel their writing and to enrich themselves. It is clearly ludicrous to say that a writer should write only positive things about her country, but when a writer presents such an unrelentingly dishonest picture of his country, which serves to perpetuate racist stereotyping, and says in as many ways as possible that nothing of value ever came from that country, then s/he is in fact saying that s/he is not of that country. It is, to my mind, a form of matricide. I go further— it is a form of pimping of the worst order, for first you destroy your place of origin and then you market your version of the destruc-

tion to those very forces that have played a part in that destruction. We cannot, for instance, and ought not to, forget the role
that the Canadian banking industry has played in the Caribbean,
in siphoning off profits from that part of the world.

Why the accolades for this work and this writer here in
Canada? In a publicity memo from Macmillan, Bissoondath's
publishers, there appears a quotation from the *Times Literary
Supplement* on the writer's first book, *Digging Up The Mountains*,
a collection of short stories. "An accomplished first collection,"
the quotation reads. What Macmillan conveniently omitted was
that the *TLS* also wrote in that very review that if Neil
Bissoondath could learn to control his racism, he might someday
become a good writer. *Digging Up The Mountains* was the same
work that garnered unqualified praise from critics in Canada. If
we understand how this society works, we should not be
surprised at the reception of this writer's works. Stanley R.
Barrett in his work, *Is God a Racist?* writes:

[R]acism in Canada has been institutionalized... racism in this
country is as deeply rooted as that in the United States... it remains
puzzling how Canadians have been able to maintain a reputation
for tolerance and harmony. What has characterized Canada has
been an ostrich-like denial that a significant problem of racial
hostility exists at all.

A work like *A Casual Brutality*, and writers who mouth the
sort of sentiments Bissoondath does, help fuel powerful myths
in this country, myths that help to perpetuate the belief system
that coming to Canada is the solution for one's problems, and
the corollary of that, that colonialism and neo-colonialism are
over and were not really problems in any event. We need,

however, to remind ourselves that contrary to the messages we receive, value and success are not one and the same thing. In his work, *On Moral Fiction*, John Gardner writes:

The lost artist is not hard to spot. Either he puts his money on texture— stunning effects, fraudulent and adventitious novelty, rant— or he puts all his money on some easily achieved or faked structure, *some melodramatic opposition of bad and good which can by nature handle only trite ideas.* [my emphasis]

A *Casual Brutality* and its author fall squarely within this description.

3086: *The Colour Purple*

A Site Report

THE YEAR IS 3086 A.D. Archaeologists sift through the rubble of a now defunct American "civilization." Among the detritus of an extinct people, they come upon a time capsule containing, among other things, books, films, newspapers, magazines and other cultural artifacts. Among the books is *The Colour Purple*; among the films is *The Colour Purple*; among the newspapers and magazines are several reviews and articles about *The Colour Purple* and its author, Alice Walker, as well as Alice Walker postcards, posters and diaries.

The archaeologists face the fundamental and perennial problem— that of constructing the life of an extinct people from the material remains of their culture. They are fortunate in finding the time capsule— unlike most archaeological finds its contents have been preserved intact.

Based on their findings, what conclusions would they be encouraged to draw about *The Colour Purple*— book and film; about Blacks and whites in North American society? What would they conclude about literature written by Blacks and its reception in North American society in the last quarter of the twentieth century?

Several qualities distinguish the archaeological find: separation in time from its original context; a monetary value inflated beyond its intrinsic worth, often due to it being the only one, or one of a few, of its kind; and a distorted aesthetic value, arbitrarily assigned by the society excavating and curating the artifact, which bears little relation to the value initially assigned to it by the society which originally produced it.

From the publication of the book to the release of the film, and its aftermath of praise and condemnation, what has happened to *The Colour Purple* and its author, has resulted in imbuing them both with the same qualities of the archaeological find— separation from context, an inflated monetary value, and an arbitrary assignment of aesthetic value.

The archaeological approach is valid in yet another way. Seldom, if ever, is Black culture and society considered a part of mainstream American culture (this applies in Canada as well); it is seen rather as some sort of exotic appendage— never understood from the inside. To consider this book, therefore, from the distanced perspective of the archaeologist, is to capture and reflect how most white readers, knowing little of Black life or culture, will or have considered it. Black readers might object to this approach, but the book has been marketed for a specific white North American market, and I am more interested in analyzing how its contents enabled, if not colluded with, this process, and how "minority" literature can be manipulated to keep certain myths intact. What has happened to *The Colour Purple* and the reasons for this are, in my opinion, far more noteworthy and significant than the book itself.

For those who have not yet either read the book, or seen the movie, *The Colour Purple* is an epistolary novel: it opens with a letter to God describing the rape of a 14-year-old girl by her stepfather; it closes with one addressed to "God, stars, trees, sky, peoples, Everything and God," which thanks God for bringing the writer's sister and children home. Between those two letters unfolds the life story of Celie, a young southern Black girl, over a period of some thirty-five years. Both those letters are hers. Through many, many more she records the loss of her two children, removed at birth by her stepfather, as well as the forced labour at the hands of her husband, Albert, who beats her, is insensitive to her sexual needs, and considers her one of the ugliest people he has ever seen. She becomes emotionally and sexually involved with Albert's mistress, Shug, and through that relationship is able to make fundamental changes in her life.

The media have presented Alice Walker and *The Colour Purple* so as to eclipse, if not obliterate, the long and distinguished literary history of the Black peoples of America, as well as the present abundance of very good or excellent Black American writers, of which she is but one. Reading the reviews, observing the extent and nature of the media coverage which, very subtly, uses her race and its "shock" value to market her, one could very easily forget that the tradition of Black writing in the United States goes all the way back to the young African slave poet, Phyllis Wheatley.

The American media are unable to deal with more than one Black superstar at any one point in time— consider for example the Michael Jackson phenomenon. Alice Walker's saleability is in part generated by her continued "uniqueness"; to link her with or make her a part of the tradition that produced Zora Neale Hurston, Toni Morrison, Ntozake Shange, Gwendolyn Brooks (another Pulitzer Prize winner), June Jordan or Paule Marshall— to name a few sister writers, would be to reduce that "uniqueness" and thereby lessen her saleability. The result is the marketing of a Black writer as a one-of-a-kind, first-of-a-kind phenomenon. For the most part, no attempt is made to put her into a context of a tradition of either American writing (and there is a noticeable American theme in the work)— she's Black so that is denied her— or Black literature. I say for the most part, for the *Nation* did say that "*The Colour Purple* place[d] her in the company of Faulkner."

I would hazard, however, based on a most inaccurate survey of TTC readers observed reading *The Colour Purple*, that most of them would not have heard of, let alone read, any of the writers mentioned above.

The overall result of this process, therefore, is a book and its author that, in the media at least, have become archaeological artifacts truly distanced in time, isolated from their source, and lacking a nexus.

To the archaeologist of 3086 a more immediate problem would have presented itself: identifying the audience— of both the author and those marketing her. They are not necessarily the same. She, the archaeologist, might conclude that the intended audience of the author was Black— she is Black and the characters are Black. Talking about the making of the film, Alice Walker says, "So much of my constituency just doesn't read, people in other countries, in Africa, who can't read English. I know that people in my hometown (Eaton, Georgia) might not read the book."[1] There is no doubt in my mind whom Alice Walker *hopes* will read her book or see the film, and nothing that I have read convinces me that Black folk, literate and illiterate were not her intended audience.

Reviews and coverage, however, have ranged from *Essence*, a magazine for and about Black women, to the *New York Times Book Review*, the bellwether of the hard-nosed competitive journalism industry; in between those, most of the reviews and articles have appeared in the white media. Unless the archaeologist has done some very good historical detective work, she would have no way of even identifying the discrepancy— that although this book was, in all likelihood, written with a Black audience in mind, it and its author were aggressively marketed for the white feminist, North American audience. This is also an audience which, over the last few years, has become aware of, and is guilty about the absence of Black women's voices and those of women of colour in the feminist movement. And where there is guilt, there will be found susceptibility to manipulation. The lesbian relationship between Shug and Celie also played a part in attracting and solidifying a lesbian readership within that movement.

Even in 1986, the only clue for me as to the identity of the targeted audience is the personal observation that the book has always had more appeal for white women than Black women, especially the latter from countries other than the United States. The marketing industry, selling Alice Walker and *The Colour Purple*, cannot, however, be solely faulted for this; were the book not amenable to this kind of marketing it would not have been possible.

Our archaeologist of 3086 might also be able to spot the role of timing in the success of the book: in 1976 a book about a poor Southern Black girl finding herself through a lesbian relationship, would have fallen with a thump, and been remaindered before the printer's ink was dry. The same story, in 1996, would probably lack shock value and be passé.

The award of the Pulitzer Prize to Alice Walker for *The Colour Purple* has so elevated it and its author, that canonization of both was the inevitable result. Undoubtedly this has had a positive effect on her financial worth as an author, and parallels may be drawn between this process and what I have earlier described as the elevated monetary value of the archaeological object.

The book is not without literary merit, let me hasten to say— quite the contrary. It is at times a beautifully written, deceptively simple work. Its African section is, however, particularly weak, and reads at times like a travelogue— a bad one at that— of Africa, with the language of these letters lacking the vitality of Celie's letters.

There are, however, reasons why the work was a "suitable" choice for the Pulitzer Prize: none of the stereotypes assigned to American Blacks— male (loutish brutes with a predilection to rape) or female (passive and mule-like) were successfully challenged. The historical underpinnings of Celie's world were noticeably absent, resulting in an aura of historical amnesia surrounding the work, and finally, the work reinforced the classic American theme of individual struggle as the solution for systemic poverty, with individual achievement and success the reward.

It would be crass and inaccurate to suggest that *The Colour Purple* was awarded the Pulitzer Prize merely because of these qualities. What we have is a book of literary merit; an ideology that needs to be seen as liberal and democratic (*any* writer can win the Pulitzer Prize), and a system that does not reward its critics; between these factors the interplay is subtle and modulated. *The Colour Purple* won the Pulitzer Prize because it *is* a good book; it is, in part, a good book because of the conformist qualities mentioned above.

Dealing with the first of these conformist qualities: Alice Walker did not set out to malign or stereotype her people: I believe she was calling the shots as she saw them. Men of all colours and stripes have been beating women and children and committing incest ever since they knew they could get away with it; that has been a very long time and race has had nothing to do with it. There have always been people— too often women— like Celie who have colluded in their own oppression— again the factor of race is irrelevant.

The critical element here, however, is audience: a Black audience knows that we are not more or less inclined to abuse or to love than other people. A white audience, especially in North America, does not, and has in fact been taught, led and encouraged to believe the opposite, and therein lies the problem for the Black writer in North America. The relative paucity of our numbers means that although we may write for a Black audience, our readership will often be other than that. In that gap created by the cross-over potential, the possibility for misunderstanding and exploitation (as discussed earlier) is great.

The second of the conformist tendencies is present in the portrayal of Celie's world— an almost discrete enclave— completely unmediated by the actions of a larger white society. Those readers aware of the extent of white America's oppression of Black people at that time can, as active readers, hold that as a backdrop to the story. When the one incidence of contact between these two societies— Black and white— occurs, resulting in the incarceration of Sofia, this incident can then be interpreted and understood within the context of the lynchings, burnings, and other activities of the Ku Klux Klan, integral to that time and place. Many whites, ignorant of that history— particularly those outside the United States— would be in no better position than our archaeologist of 3086 trying to locate the book in some sort of social and historical context.

The historical amnesia of *The Colour Purple* places it squarely within the ahistorical traditions of America— a new world established in supposed opposition to the old, and free of all the historical baggage that continued to entrap the latter. We all know where that particular myth has taken us.

Is it fair to ask an author to write the book she didn't intend to? No, but I have as much difficulty with the absence of a wider social and historical context in the deep South of the forties, as I would have with a book about Jews set in Germany of the forties that omitted reference to the German state.

The last of the conformist themes is visible in Celie's transformation to a small business entrepreneur, having worked her way up and out from Southern poverty. The message— in blackface— is a variation on the theme of "anybody can be President of the United States— provided you work hard." (No one bothers to add that being white and male is a decided advantage.) It is a profoundly American theme and fantasy, and an ideal which most Blacks in Celie's world would not have been able to realize.

The Colour Purple is now being touted as *the* book about *the* Black experience; Alice Walker as *the* best Black writer: *The New York Times Magazine*, January 8, 1984, titled their article about her, "Novelist Alice Walker: Telling *the* Black Woman's Story" [my emphasis]. The specific has become the general, and this particular story, rooted in a particular time and history, albeit absent from the book, now becomes *the* Black woman's story. The Black woman's story is many, and much more differentiated and nuanced than this.

In part, the absence of the historically specific spawns this sort of generalising, but as with the archaeological process, what we have is the arbitrary assignment of certain values to a work that has little to do with the variety of Black societies or cultures.

These latter play no part in the assignment of an aesthetic value
to Alice Walker or *The Colour Purple*. Such decisions are made
in New York or San Francisco— not Eaton, Georgia.

The plethora of objects associated with *The Colour Purple*—
post cards, posters, diaries, might encourage our archaeologist
to assume the presence of a cult that generated extreme veneration. If she truly understood the post-nuclear, post-feminist,
capitalism-in-crisis societies of the second half of the eighties, she
might understand that what was being worshipped was only an
image and that true veneration was held for the American dollar.

A few comments about the film: it is the logical and expected
development of the themes in the book, so those who criticize
the treatment of Black males in the film have only to look to the
book for the source.

In fairness to Alice Walker, the book traced the decline *and*
moral redemption of the men much more clearly and definitively
than does the film. The moral message is very clear in the book,
and a balance, lacking in the film, is maintained. Unfortunately,
in this case, the power of the visual image of film has been
harnessed to capture, irrevocably, the brutality of the Black male.

Like the book, the African scenes are weak and exotic: an
African scarification ceremony, for instance, is juxtaposed with
a scene of Celie about to slit her husband's throat! I don't now
what our archaeologist will make of that— that African scarification ceremonies are crimes?

Alice Walker is quoted as saying, "Well, if he (Steven
Speilberg) can do Martians, maybe he can do us."[2] She was closer
to the truth than she probably realized. This throwaway statement reinforces what I said earlier about Blacks being perceived
as being distant and apart from American society— aliens always.

The making of the film reinforces all the issues mentioned

above: the one-of-a-kind syndrome; inflated monetary values and a distorted aesthetic value assigned, in this case, by Speilberg wanting to make a "serious" film.

I doubt that this review will be among those found in the time capsule, but the very issue that will confront our archaeologist of 3086 confronts me now: who is the audience of this particular article— Blacks or whites and does that matter? Were such a piece to be found in the capsule, our archaeologist might well ask about the merits of a Black writer criticizing the work of another Black writer in a forum that is predominantly white. I could cop out and reply that, given that the book's audience is a predominantly white one, there is no better forum, but it is a cop out, and one that does not address the hard questions: who *is* our audience; whom do we wish to hear us and respond; who markets us and why; how do we earn a living doing what we do best, when our intended audience is limited in numbers, buying power or literacy?

There are no easy solutions to these issues; by 3086 they might all have been solved— finally, but suffice it to say to all writers, Black and white, writing athwart the mainstream, the marketing of *The Colour Purple* is instructive to all of us— co-optation is an extremely attractive and risky business.

END NOTES:

1. *Ms. Magazine*, December, 1985.
2. Ibid.

Gut Issues in Babylon

Racism & Anti-Racism in the Arts

THE GUT! IS WHERE I EXPERIENCE RACISM. When a newspaper vendor throws my change at me, simply because I'm Black, I feel it in my gut; when I hear of the shooting of a young boy in the back of the head, and know in my bones, before I hear it on the radio, that he is Black, it is my gut that twists and turns; when an agent who has been trying to market my books, tells me that publishers are not even interested in reading the manuscript because it features Black children, my gut tightens and wrenches. And when I read of the appallingly unscientific and racist theories of Phillippe Rushton of the University of Western Ontario, my immediate gut response is that he should be eliminated. By any means necessary.

My heart then aches for my people and the centuries of unrelenting attacks upon our persons and our humanity, my head buzzes with the effort of trying to think my way out of the morass or racism. And *somehow* I must contain my gut revulsion for these theories and for this man and his kind. I must bring to bear on what is, in my opinion, a carefully orchestrated plan against African peoples,[1] as carefully thought-out and as rigorously articulated reasons why individuals such as he, and ideologies such as he espouses, should be excoriated from any society of humans we wish to take pride in.

My body and its body intelligence— I include the mind in this concept— are deeply involved and implicated in the practice of racism— against me and others— even though I personally may never be physically attacked. Remembering— I have never forgotten!— that it was for our bodies that we were first brought to this brave New World, the irony of this observation does not escape me.

"Would you let your daughter marry a Black man?" While this question has entered the realm of cliché, it is hard to get more gut than that. The image— it is, perhaps, more appropriate to say nightmare— conjured up of the white man's daughter in "the gross clasps of a lascivious Moor" (Shakespeare, Othello) making the "great two-backed beast" strikes at the heart of white patriarchy— white women being mounted by Black men who are, as we all know and as has recently been "corroborated" by Mr. Rushton, proverbially better endowed. When we lay aside the veneer of scholarship and specious research, how clearly the gut issue presents itself, how efficiently it has hidden itself.

As it ripples out from the centre— from the gut— racism multiplies exponentially and indefinitely, until it thoroughly permeates the bureaucracies, the institutions, the arts, culture, education— the entire society; until it becomes exceedingly difficult to find the gut issue.

Racism is a gut issue. Because it is a gut issue, it is an explosive and, at times, a murderous issue. Because racism is a gut issue it is a difficult issue to solve, particularly so when it metastasizes quickly and efficiently into the facelessness of systemic racism, apparently evacuated of any guts.

When I first conceived the idea for this article, I intended to do a piece on anti-racism and the arts. The kernel of the idea arose from a situation that had developed in 1988 at a feminist publishing house in Toronto, The Women's Press, and which gave rise to issues of racism and anti-racist publishing. The crisis at this press touched— directly or indirectly— most women writers in Toronto, if not Canada. I was one of the writers whose work had been accepted for publication in the anthology that catalyzed the crisis, and was, over several months, the recipient— at times it felt like the target— of a great deal of correspondence by the two groups that developed at the Press. The issue came to the fore at the Third International Feminist Book Fair in 1988, which itself had to confront issues of racism in its organizing of the fair.

My desire to look at the arts in general was an attempt, on my part, to broaden the issue. I wished to move the debate away from The Women's Press and the writer-and-voice/censorship debate that had swirled, seemingly interminably, around this very particular set of circumstances, affecting this particular publishing house when it attempted to grapple with racism and establish some sort of corrective to it. I wanted to look at how other arts disciplines and organizations were, if at all, dealing with racism. Once I had, however, identified the gut nature of racism, I had to ask myself whether I too, in taking this approach, was not attempting to move away too quickly from what the gut issue was for me— racism, the very issue that had propelled me in the first place, to look at other arts groups and disciplines. I had to return to the gut.

The gut issue for me, an African Caribbean woman holding a Canadian passport (the Ben Johnson lesson is a chastening one), attempting to make a living as a writer in Toronto, was that The Women's Press had never published a work by a Black woman— or any other woman of colour, for that matter— in its then 16 year history. It *was* a gut issue when they appeared singularly uninterested in the manuscript of a novel I submitted to them some years ago.[2] And it certainly was a gut issue when in 1985, or thereabouts, a proposed anthology of writings by Black women to be published by The Women's Press, gave rise to criticisms by members of the Press that much of the writing was anthropological or, in one case, not Black enough!

When, in 1987, The Women's Press approached me to submit a piece for their anthology on feminist theory, *Works in Progress*, I challenged them as to why I was to be the only Black woman in the collection: was this not, in fact, tokenism, I argued to the editor, and further, how much of the other work in the collection would address the differing realities of Black women or women of colour?[3] This was a gut issue for me, and so was the identical situation raised by their subsequent approach to me again in 1987 for a piece of fiction to be included in their anthology *Imagining Women*. Once again, I raised the issue of lack of representation of *all* women and provided them with a list of names of African and Asian writers from whom they should attempt to solicit submissions. *Imagining Women* would be the catalyst that eventually precipitated the split in The Women's Press— the irony does not escape me.

To sum up, African Canadian women writers— the only group on whose behalf I may presume, albeit tentatively, to speak, did not view The Women's Press as a particularly friendly place for their work. It was, in my opinion, no different from the other mainstream presses. Correction— there was one difference: they held themselves out as being feminist and therefore representative of *all* women, when in fact they represented a very specific group— white, middle class women. And to be brutally frank, when the issue of racism exploded at the Press and became public, my first gut response was: "It's about time— they've had it coming for a long time!" I was to think the same thing as I watched the city convulse over racism over the last few months. It's about time. Except that we get killed and that is a gut issue.

No one was killed at The Women's Press, but there were casualties: some of these had to with individuals losing their jobs, some to do with the loss of a certain reputation previously held by The Women's Press among the various literary and publishing networks around the country. Certain bookstores and distributors have, for instance, since refused to carry the Press' books. The response of various organizations as well as the media appears to have focused on two issues: the behaviour of those members of the Press who perceived themselves as taking an anti-racist stand, and the issue of censorship. In the ensuing debate which the media— print and electronic— have covered, racism has remained a non-issue.

Without wanting to dwell unduly on a situation that has already been debated excessively both in and out of the media, my limited understanding of the facts that precipitated the crisis at The Women's Press in the summer of 1988 is as follows: three short stories for the proposed anthology *Imagining Women* were rejected by the Publishing and Policy Group (PPG) after they had been accepted by the fiction manuscript committee. The reason given by the PPG was that the stories were either explicitly or implicitly racist. The two issues that arose from this action on the part of the PPG were: (a) whether the PPG had the right to reject material already accepted by the manuscript committee; and (b) whether the stories were, in fact, racist. Opinions diverged radically on both issues and eventually led to the splitting up of the Press.

The Women's Press dispute saw the coming together of two gut issues— power and racism— making the situation doubly explosive. What happened at The Women's Press was, in my opinion, essentially a power struggle among white women that manifested itself in the issue of racism— it could have arisen over any other issue. That was what my gut told me after attending one public meeting. The fact that racism, as an issue, has remained subsidiary to that of censorship, or writer-and-voice, confirms for me the general reluctance in Canadian society to tackle this issue. This may appear a harsh opinion; I cannot, however, conclude otherwise in view of the fact that when the issue of racism in writing and publishing finally surfaced, the debate would not be about how to ensure that African, Native, or Asian women have access to the publishing resources of a feminist press, but about whether white middle class women ought or ought not to be allowed, or should be able, to use the voice of traditionally oppressed groups!

It is tempting to dismiss the whole matter as ludicrous. It remains, however, a gut issue for me. The unarticulated assumption behind the Press' Anti-Racist Guidelines, put out in the summer of 1988, and designed to tell *white* women how to write in a non-racist way, was that their writers would also be white. At no time were the Anti-Racist Guidelines allied to an affirmative action publishing policy, such as a commitment that the Press would, if necessary, help develop manuscripts by African, Asian, or Native women writers, as well as publish a certain number of books by such authors annually, or by a certain date. Both sides are implicated in this charade. The Press' more recent Anti-Racist Guidelines for Submissions, stating that the Press "will publish fiction and non-fiction work by women of colour on issues determined by their concerns," represents a small movement in the direction of an affirmative action publishing policy.

I do not for one moment suggest that individuals at The Women's Press were not, or are not, serious about the eradication of racism— quite the contrary— but I do feel that there was insufficient consulting with a wide enough range of writers— African, Asian, and Native— to ensure that the views of the very groups on behalf of whom some members were advocating were adequately represented.

On the rare occasion when a white person attempted to voice what "women of colour" wanted, there was the unfortunate tendency to assign a monolithic nature to African, Asian, and Native Canadians by "selecting" one or two individuals who spoke "on behalf of" the entire group. This is a dangerous and pernicious practice, particularly now that anti-racism has become a growth industry. These groups are, in fact, no more monolithic than are white groups: to see them as such is an expression of racism.

Very simply put, my opinion is that if every white writer were, voluntarily or otherwise, to decide not to write from the point of view of African, Asian or Native women, this would in no way ensure access to publication by these latter women. Such action would do nothing to ensure that our work was reviewed or taken by distributors or even taken seriously. Such simple proscriptions are hollow victories.

There is, however, a grievous crime— I use those words advisedly— that certain members of The Women's Press and the Anti-Racist Guidelines attempted to address. The crime is that for centuries and for far too long, white European cultures have penetrated other cultures. Where Europeans have not pillaged they have looted; and while doing these things they have, wantonly or otherwise, destroyed centuries of learning and knowledge. They have barbarized civilizations and cultures; where, because they needed the labour, they declined to wipe out entire peoples, they have appropriated their labour, or the product of that labour along with whatever they considered valuable.

The examples of this exploitation are legion, but a couple of outrageous ones will suffice. To begin at the beginning— at least for Westerners— there is a growing body of white mainstream scholarship which reveals that the so-called "cradle of civilization," Greece, "significantly borrowed culturally [and] linguistically from Egypt and Phonecia."[4] And whether we accept, as some scholars do— Ali Mazrui for instance–[5] that Africans, along with other races, contributed to Egyptian civilization, or remain, like Cheik Anta Diop,[6] the late Senegalese intellectual, convinced that Egypt was primarily an African civilization, the fact remains that Egyptians were the cultural ancestors of the Greeks. The obliteration of this fact, as Martin Bernal argues in Black Athena,[7] is directly attributable to the rise of racism in the nineteenth century.

The second example has to do with art and modernism. That the modernist movement in art is heir to African aesthetics is indisputable, yet beginning with Picasso, the movement's most famous pioneer, most of these artists eventually denied any African influence on their work. Some, like Brancusi, even went to the extreme of destroying their earlier work because it appeared "too African."

What really twists the gut, however, is that when artists from African cultures attempt to gain an audience for their work in metropolitan areas, the doors swiftly close. If and when the work is shown, as in the case of Wilfredo Lam, the Afro-Cuban artist, whose work, *The Jungle*, is on display at the MOMA, it is shown as an appendage to the work of the European, in this case Picasso. Lam's work, in fact, hangs in the hallway leading to the museum's coat room; the commentary by the museum's curator suggests that it is an homage to Picasso's "Les Demoiselles d'Avignon."[8]

For the white artist/writer/painter/musician— particularly the male of the species— the world is his oyster, and if he wishes to use Asian, African or Native culture in his work, then why the hell not? What does white mean, if it does not mean being able to lay waste and lay claim to anything you may happen to set your mind to? That is the moral turpitude at the heart of white "civilization." The *mea culpas* are long overdue.

That was the gut issue— the apparent freedom of whites to appropriate as their own whatsoever they wished— to which The Women's Press guidelines attempted to offer a corrective. The guidelines could be seen as both a *mea culpa* and an attempt to right a wrong. And while I do not advocate, for reasons too many to enter into here, proscriptions against writers writing from voices other than their own, The Women's Press *must* be given credit for their courage in tackling this issue, albeit not in the most effective way. In a society such as ours, where there has been an "ostrich-like denial that a significant problem of racial hostility exists at all,"[9] such actions are significant; the opportunities they present for sound anti-racist work ought not to be minimized.

ANTI-RACISM

SEXISM IS TO RACISM as feminism is to civil rights? multiculturalism? Black Power? anti-racism? None of those suggestions is

satisfactory, and the difficulty in finding the word that corre-
sponds with feminism is linked to some of the difficulty around
the concept of anti-racism. Were we to be entirely accurate when
talking about discrimination practised by one racial group
against the other, the appropriate word would be "racialism" and
not "racism." Usage has, however, determined that racism is the
word that has come to encapsulate that particular practice; it
includes and embraces both the individual type of discrimination, as typified by the landlord who refuses to rent his apartment
to an Indian, as well as the more elaborate philosophies, such
as those espoused by Rushton, of white supremacist movements.

The absence of a word that parallels feminism is significant.
Sexism refers to the practice of patriarchy; feminism, or woman-
ism as some Black women have chosen to re-define it, to a
movement that seeks to empower women through any number
of ways. To be feminist or womanist would, I assume, at least
imply that one was anti-sexist, and I would argue that contained
within the concept of feminism is the practice of anti-sexism.
However, while books, policies and workplaces may be anti-sexist, the term feminism means more than being anti-sexist. There
is an element of the positive, the proactive, the celebratory
implied in the use of the word: feminism is not only *against*
sexism, but in favour of, in support of, in celebration of
something.

There was a time when the concept of Black Power would
have paralleled feminism, in both its proactive and reactive
aspects; a time when those words encapsulated an entire philosophy built on Black pride and initiative, while also being against
the practice of racism. Those words also, if we are to be honest,
struck fear into the hearts of those who ruled.

Eventually, the words would become too closely associated with the Black armed struggle, with the Black Panthers, and with the threat they presented to the government of the United States; eventually the words would be evacuated of their more celebratory aspects such as the insistence on the creation of our own images, or the recognition of the beauty of those who had been defined as Other for too long. A very simple, and yet not so simple, thing like an Afro— Angela Davis', for instance— came to symbolize a revolution long overdue. But that was long before the flight from Black, as I call it.

There was a time when Black was a political colour. The late Walter Rodney, the Guyanese intellectual, argues its meaning brilliantly in *The Grounding with My Brothers*. His argument is that during their expansionist and imperialist periods, much of the treatment meted out by the European nations to the world's peoples of colour was similar. Despite differences in culture, colour, language and location, what these countries and peoples shared was the fact that they were not white-skinned which, in turn, guaranteed their exploitation:

If a Jamaican Black man tried to get a room from a landlady in London who said "No Coloured," it would not impress her if he said he was West Indian, quite apart from the fact that she would already have closed the door in his Black face. When a Pakistani goes to the Midlands, he is as coloured as a Nigerian. The Indonesian is the same as a Surinamer in Holland.[10]

The position of the peoples of African descent was, however, "clearly more acute than that of most non-white groups,"[11] he argued. It was these black-skinned ones who would lend their colour to name a movement that would attempt to re-assert a balance in the inequitable distribution of the world's resources and power— Black Power.

Black is now emptied of its political meaning. Director of the Institute for Race Relations in London, and editor of *Race and Class*, A. Sivanandan, writes that "Black from being a 'political colour' was broken down into its cultural parts of West Indian, Asian, African— and these in turn reduced to their ethnic constituents."[12] I discern no little racism in this flight, albeit the reasons given usually stress the need to emphasize one's ethnicity. The more insidious reason, I believe, is a fundamental unwillingness to be associated with Blackness or Africans. While I understand and support the need to emphasize one's ethnicity, I also observe that "white" as a political term and concept is able to encompass both the blond, blue-eyed Northerner and the dark-haired, dark-skinned Southerner. At the same time, I haven't noticed that there is any possibility of mistaking German culture for Italian culture.

Neither multiculturalism, civil or human rights meet the need for a word that contains the creative tension of opposition *against*, as well as *in celebration of*. While multiculturalism is somewhat descriptive of the ethnic composition of Canadian society, it is a bureaucratic construct and fails to address the power differential that exists among the many cultures. Civil or human rights remain what they are, legalistic descriptions of one's rights within a society allegedly governed by the rule of law.

Those who are interested in struggling for a more just society, for essentially that is what the fight against racism is all about— a struggle "against injustice, inequality, against freedom for some and un-freedom for others"[13]— must, therefore, resort to that catch-all phrase, anti-racism. The danger is that people come to believe that there exists an ideology called anti-racism. The reverse is actually more true— there is an ideology of racism which anti-racism attempts to combat in as many different ways as there are manifestations of racism. As Sivanandan writes:

There is no body of thought called anti-racism, no orthodoxy, or dogma, no manual of strategy and tactics, no demonology. What there was in our society was racism, in every walk of life, and it had to be opposed— in every conceivable way. And because racism was hydra-headed, and reared its different heads in different ways in different times (prosperity and depression) and differing relations (employment, housing, schools) and different places (inner city, suburbia), the ways of fighting racism were also different and legion. Nor were there any short-cuts to its demise. Racism had been a long time in the making and would take a long time to die. "Anti-racism," therefore, was a portmanteau word meant to carry all these differing ideas and ways of combating racism. The important thing, however, was to keep racism from corrupting society to decay.[14]

Anti-racism then comes to include both reactive and proactive actions— actions like the Anti-Racist Guidelines put out by The Women's Press, which were essentially reactive, as well as more proactive measures such as affirmative action publishing strategies. To develop these strategies we move from the gut to the head, but I would argue the need always to remember that racism is, and always will be, a gut issue. Anyone who felt that Toronto, or Canada for that matter, did not have a racial problem, should have had that belief laid to rest over the last few months. Racism is alive and well and kicking shit in Toronto, in Ontario and all over Canada. All of which brings me to the arts.

THE CULTURAL FACES OF RACISM

AS MENTIONED EARLIER, my intention was to look at the arts in general to see whether there had been any attempts made to identify the practice of racism, and to deal with it as The Women's Press had attempted to do. To recognize the anti-racist practices or solutions instituted within a particular discipline, it was first necessary to identify the nature of racism in each discipline. What follows is an overview of the cultural faces of racism in dance, theatre, music, literature, film and video. This overview is by no means intended to be an exhaustive analysis of all that is happening in those disciplines with respect to racism; nor does it deal with institutions like A Space or other artist-run centres, or organizations which deserve an entire article devoted to their practices. I was, and am, particularly interested in how Black[15] artists perceive their particular disciplines; how racism impinges on them and how they continue to practise their art under such limitations.

I have also looked at the primary funding agencies, since their funding policies and, in particular, their understanding of racism and approach to anti-racism directly affect the survival of Black and other artists of colour. With a view to taking the pulse of professional organizations, I also looked briefly at two related to writing. As a writer I confess to being particularly interested in these two groups.

I intend the results of my inquiries to be essentially a spring board for further inquiry by artists themselves, by funding organizations and other interested arts groups. By presenting the information as I have done, in appendix form, the reader will, I hope, be able to grasp quickly the overwhelming and appalling similarity of the systemic racism that permeates the disciplines I looked at. The reader can, as well, for comparison purposes, follow a particular area such as training or funding through all the disciplines.

Racism will, depending on the discipline, manifest itself differently in each area. While the Black writer, for instance, may have to deal with funding agencies, she also has to deal with the marketplace and the censorship of the marketplace that occurs through racism. The Black documentary filmmaker, on the other hand, deals primarily with institutions such as the National Film Board; her existence as a documentary filmmaker is much more dependent on such sources of institutional funding than is the writer's. The former can, after all, always publish her work herself and, as some writers have done, market it herself. Fundamentally, however, the core of racism in the arts remains constant: the refusal to treat as valid the cultural experience, knowledge or expertise of the Black artist, wedded to the belief that Eurocentric values are, in and of themselves, better.

Because racism can be a debilitating experience, it is important that while identifying it, we also record the ingenuity of individuals and groups in getting around, or over, the hurdles created by racism, so that they can continue to practise their art. The solutions which I have identified are, therefore, as important as the problems I have uncovered. Many of these solutions may be seen as reactive to the wide practice of racism in the arts, but in a Black theatre group mounting its own show, for instance, or a Black publisher publishing a work by a Black writer, the proactive nature of such anti-racist practices is visible.

The results of my investigation appear in the appendix at the end of this piece.

COMMENTARY

ARTS COUNCILS ARE NOT THE ONLY institutions to practise the highly developed art of racism by neglect; the councils are, however, important since their funding of particular projects serve as virtual stamps of approval, and sends a message throughout the arts community. While the composition of juries, for instance, remains in its present scandalous state with little or no expertise or resources to assess African-based dance, for example, or work coming out of the linguistic traditions of the Caribbean, racism will continue to flourish in the councils. I maintain that provided the will is there, the composition of juries and panels remains one area where changes can be made most easily.

Within the general marketplace, I would like to see those institutions and businesses like dance companies and publishing houses which receive federal monies having to report both on their employment equity programmes, *as well as* on their inclusion of *all* artists, Black and white, in their shows and publications. I have no illusion as to the resistance such a proposal will engender in the art world, but if, however, such companies will not change voluntarily, then changes will have to be induced legally.

The energy and talent of Black artists in the face of overwhelming odds is demonstrable; this must now be matched by the funding bodies, by the arts organizations and by the marketplace.

WHA' FE DO (WHAT TO DO)

WHEN I CONSIDER THE RESPONSES to my inquiries by the funding bodies, all of which are, for the most part, serious and well-meaning, and consider in turn the depth and apparent intransigence of the racism as revealed in the appendix below, it is difficult not to grow weary. When I hear that in 1988 the reason given for not hiring Black musicians is that they cannot read music, it is difficult, if not impossible, not to feel that one is living in a time warp. The divide between the lived reality of the Black artist, and the funding policies of arts councils, between the Black artist and the art world in general is so great as to be almost unbridgeable.

Automatic and almost instinctive, the response to the Black artist and her work by the art world is one that reveals a profound lack of respect for the individual artist and her cultural traditions, particularly when she, and not a white artist, is the practitioner of these traditions. The flip side of this response is the cultural appropriation by the white artist of those very traditions for his or her personal aggrandizement. And therein lies the gut issue. It is clear that the arts councils have not even begun to address the issue of racism, relying instead on the practices surrounding the concept of multiculturalism.[16] While I am not suggesting that multiculturalism be abandoned, I see no reason why multiculturalism *and* anti-racism need be mutually exclusive.

I STARTED OUT THIS ESSAY by talking about the gut issue of racism— for me at least. I suspect that for the individual white person the gut issue is going to be giving up of some of the power and privilege they have held for so long, and learning to view as equals those whom they have long considered inferiors. And herein lies the significance of Rushton's theories for white supremacists of all shades.

What I am talking about is not an easy thing to do or accomplish. I am not even sure that it's possible. Many well-meaning individuals, eager to do the right thing, believe that by including the odd multicultural writer in a curriculum, for instance, or tinkering here and there with superficialities, what is needed will be accomplished. What is necessary goes much deeper than these cosmetic changes and will be profoundly disturbing for many.

On a personal level, the eradication of racism will require, at least, a complete rethinking of one's values so that one does not automatically equate white with better and/or more desirable; it must mean an understanding of one's privilege as the purveyor of certain cultural representations, and the cost of that to others; it should mean an understanding of the political and social underpinnings of what we have come to know as knowledge; it ought to mean an understanding of how, in a racist society, traditions such as scientific objectivity and academic freedom become tainted and are used as shields for racists. It means, above all, not just a shift in one's perspectives, but a shift in the position *from which* one's perspective is formed. What it means is at times gut-wrenching, gut-twisting change. And who wants to do that? It is far easier to yield to the forces of inertia; turn on the TV and leave things as they are.

On a systemic level such change must mean the institution and enactment of affirmative action policies *on all levels* in the art world, from the marketplace to the arts councils; from the performance spaces to the classrooms.

We live in a society in which our mode of thinking is one of binary opposition: the either/or conundrum. My life or your

death. My well-being or your lack of well-being; my wealth or
your poverty. Closely tied to this is the concept of scarcity, real
or contrived, which is essential to the proper functioning of
capitalist societies. We are continually encouraged, by various
means, to believe that the satisfaction of one person's needs
automatically means the non-fulfilment of another's. White
middle class female writers, therefore, come to believe that the
publication of works by Black and other writers of colour,
automatically means the non-publication of their works. Scarcity,
wedded to binary oppositional thought, results in a deadly
combination: policy makers and arts councils come to believe
that the funding of works by African, Asian and Native artists
must be at the expense of mainstream cultural representation;
the flip side of this is the belief that the only way to ensure that
European culture continues to flourish is to deprive non-European artists of adequate funding.

This specious— I am tempted to say magical— belief in
scarcity is as powerful as it is unwarranted: there is no doubt in
my mind that European cultural representation can exist alongside cultural representation by African, Asian and Native artists.
We would all be culturally richer for it as well. But the fear that
scarcity engenders— that the metaphorical pie is not big enough
for us all to share— is what drives many to hold on to privilege.

In view of all the forces massed against profound and
meaningful change, not the least of which are the powerful
media, any change which does take place will happen piecemeal,
in eruptions here and there as in The Women's Press ordeal, or
in small epiphanic moments as it did for some in the aftermath
of that event. But happen it must.

James Baldwin wrote that, "Not everything that is faced can
be changed, but nothing can be changed until it is faced." Racism

might never be eradicated, but it certainly will *not* be eradicated until it is faced, not once, but over and over again until we become so fed up with it, we chuck the whole damn stinking mess out.

Racism is on the rise in Toronto and in Canada. The racism that exists and flourishes in the arts is all of a piece with the racism in education, the racism in policing, and the racism in the workplace. Each of these areas has a particular significance to our society, and the significance of the arts or cultural representation cannot be emphasized too much.

It is through cultural representation that the artist re-presents the guts and soul of a people; the urge to such representation is, from all evidence, basic to the human species. The impulse to creativity and cultural re-presentation will, if stymied, continue, but in more negative ways.

While it is at times extremely difficult, I do believe— have faith in the essential improvability of the human species. I suppose I must. If I don't I may as well give up. Nadine Gordimer writes that "the writer is eternally in search of entelechy in his [sic] relation to his society." I go further; not only the writer, but the artist, the human being, the human species, is in search of perfection in its relation to society. However, while blights such as racism, sexism and classism exist, such perfection will continue to escape us.

Here in Canada, there has traditionally been a reluctance to face the ugly facts of racism— the gut issues; The Women's Press faced them and suffered many casualties as a consequence. The community of writers, and the arts community in general, have benefited tremendously from this painful, but necessary, bringing to the fore of what some of us knew was there all along. The opportunity for enlightening debate, the potential for change and yes, love or *agape*, as in the old sense of charity for one's neighbour— the West Africans call it *ashé* or supreme coolness— are all there. We ought to seize this opportunity; it might not present itself in quite this way again. Blacks and whites facing each other across flaming barricades in Toronto— this is no longer an unlikely image. I would not have said so two years ago; I hope two years hence I can read this and conclude I was crying wolf. But things must get better. Or worse. They will not remain the same.

Appendix 2

DANCE

COMMENT:
There are amazing Black dancers out there, but they don't get the exposure, and are put in the ethnic bracket.— Patricia Wynter, Dancer

TRAINING:
Dancers only trained in modern and balletic techniques; no training in or validity assigned to African techniques or African aesthetics of movement.

FUNDING:
Inadequate; African-based dance dismissed as ethnic, marginal— non-mainstream; funding based on evaluation in ballet or modern dance; no one on juries to assess the aesthetics of African dance.

PERFORMANCE:
In modern dance Black female dancers often passed over on the grounds that they do not have the appropriate body build— too much muscle is the complaint. "The Black female dancer needs to be very, very thin, slim-hipped, flat-chested and/or very exceptional." Black male dancers in some instances more easily hired because they satisfy the need for exotic elements. Very seldom paid for rehearsal time; rehearsal space scarce and expensive— particularly for groups operating on very limited resources.

SOLUTIONS:
The creation of Black/African dance companies like Usafiri, Ebony Voices, Siyaka, Chissamba Chiyuka and Sethlabi Taunyane's group. All these groups operate on shoe-string budgets.

STILL TO BE DONE:
More adequate funding for groups and individual dancers;
More representation by individuals knowledgeable in non-European dance forms on arts councils.

FILM AND VIDEO DOCUMENTARY

COMMENT:
There is pressure to make a film and video that focuses on a little bit of initiative, a little bit of organization, a little bit of dance and music and lots of progressive nostalgia, rather than serious film that will deal with the stark realities of racism, immigration and human rights from a legal and human perspective.— Premike Ratnam, Filmmaker

TRAINING:
Very low expectations of the student on the part of the teachers and fellow students; undervaluing and underestimation of student's work until another audience acknowledges it; no respect for professional competence.

FUNDING:
Traditionally inadequate; African, Asian, or Native content not seen as valid but as minority culture; work viewed as educational and non-mainstream; "Come back when you've made it" or "We made a Black film last year" are typical comments; filmmakers not allowed to move out of their ethnic or racial slot to make a film on mainstream issues like rape; funders often want to shape ethnic or racially based material according to their interests, not the interests of the filmmaker.

SALES:
Often told there is no market for work.

PRACTICE:
Appropriation of experiences by white filmmakers making films *about* Asians, Natives or Africans and often having more access to funds.

SOLUTIONS:
Resolution passed at last AGM (1988) of the Independent Film and Video Alliance that: (a) the group support in principle the right of Native groups to make film and video on Native issues; (b) that the Alliance would support film and video production by Native groups wherever necessary.

STILL TO BE DONE:
Develop among young people the awareness of careers in film and the importance of being able to control the making of images of oneself. Lobby for greater control by visible minorities over the making of images about themselves.

* It is my understanding that the reason for the recent disbanding of the NFB's Studio D unit is to increase accessibility to those who have not traditionally had adequate access to the studio, such as Native, African, Asian women or the handicapped. Whether such increased accessibility will be the result is too soon to tell at this time.

LITERATURE

COMMENT:
The fundamental problem is that in Canada the term Black Canadian is not a legitimate term, and, therefore, the aspirations of Black Canadians are viewed as intrusive rather than a natural part of the body politic. In contradistinction, despite

the racism in the U.S., Black American aspirations are seen as legitimate and not
aberrant.— Claire Harris, Poet

TRAINING:
Work of literature from non-European traditions seldom part of the
curriculum; lack of interest in creative writing programmes in issues of
language revolving around dialect and standard English.

FUNDING:
Extreme difficulty in obtaining funding by those authors choosing to work in a
demotic variant of English; insensitivity of arts councils to such linguistic
traditions; lack of interest in Black experiences often the subject matter of
work by Black authors.

PUBLISHING:
Refusal of publishers to publish works by Black authors; reluctance or refusal
on the part of media to review published works by Black authors, unless work
panders to racism or fulfils stereotypes; problems with distribution of books
by Black authors; lack of interest on the part of distributors and bookstores.

PROFESSIONAL GROUPS:
Lack of interest in Black writers or writers of colour and their concerns;
rejection of work on the grounds that it is not literature.

SOLUTIONS:
Creation of presses like Sister Vision, Williams Wallace and Carib Can with
mandates to publish work by Black and other writers of colour.

STILL TO BE DONE:
Establish affirmative actions programmes for publishing houses;
Make it mandatory that publishing houses receiving federal funds begin

reporting along with other businesses on their employment equity
programmes;
Require that publishers report annually on how many manuscripts by Black
and other minority writers they have seriously considered, as well as providing
the government with some sort of target figures for publication.

MUSIC: JAZZ AND BLUES

COMMENT:
*After so many years Black musicians seem to be still in the position of making
music without reaping the rewards.*— Diana Braithwaite, Singer/Musician

TRAINING:
Black music today taught primarily by whites in universities.

WORK:
Black musicians still doing performances— seldom get studio work which is
better paid; reasons given are that Black musicians can't read music; whites
imitate Black sound and get jobs; whites still making money on Black music;
unlike Eurocentric music no credit ever given to Black initiators of forms like
12-bar blues; blues sung by whites with no respect for tradition or feeling;
blues have crossed over to the point that white musicians can imitate sound
from traditional country blues to Chicago blues resulting in white musicians
getting more and higher paying gigs than Blacks; Blacks not sufficiently
employed in production; absence of record deals with big companies; refusal
of Juno awards to recognize the variety of Black music.

AIRPLAY:
Radio stations playing Black music seldom employ Blacks either in
programming or production.

SOLUTIONS:
The establishment of the Juno reggae music award; setting up of organizations like the Black Music Association and the Black Music Association of Canada which lobby on behalf of Black musicians.

STILL TO BE DONE:
Establish an institution where traditional Black music can be taught;
Pressure radio stations playing Black music to hire more Blacks;
Take initiative in collecting and protecting Black music;
Establish separate categories at the Juno awards for calypso and reggae.

THEATRE

COMMENT:
Content affects everything— training, funding and casting, and it's obvious that Black content is being rejected, and that is our essence; if that is being rejected we need to examine that and change it.— Ahdri Zhina Mandiela, Actor/Director

TRAINING:
Black actors trained in standard methods, what they have naturally is trained out of them.

FUNDING:
Marginalized and insufficient; work dismissed by arts councils as amateur and lacking in professionalism; work categorized as folk or ethnic.

PERFORMANCE:
Black content not considered worthy of presentation at any level; insufficient colour-blind casting in mainstream theatre; insufficient performance of scripts by Black playwrights; very little respect for quality, validity and relevance of work even by distinguished playwrights like Walcott.

SOLUTIONS:
Formation of Black theatre groups like Imani Theatre Ensemble, Theatre in the Rough, Theatre Fountainhead— all operating on shoe-string budgets; production companies like Jones and Jones; colour-blind casting companies like Emerald City.

STILL TO BE DONE:
Increase the awareness of arts councils to the aesthetic validity of the content of Black theatre;
More adequate funding for Black theatre groups;
More relevant training for young actors.

VISUAL ART

COMMENT:
We don't believe in total assimilation. We find we are not accepted in the gallery scene, even at the alternative galleries, except for A Space. It is still a struggle to stay within A Space. As artists we suffer from a lack of knowledge of the system and how it works. The upholders of the system refuse to recognize the value of other cultural artifacts. Our art is not an inferior substitute.— Busejee Bailey, Artist

TRAINING:
Emphasis on Eurocentric values and aesthetics; conservative view of cultural protection, e.g., traditional bead-work by Native women and the traditional textiles of African women dismissed as craft, except when validated through use by white artists; refusal to recognize other cultural languages.

FUNDING:
Failure of arts councils to accept responsibility for cultural representation; marginalized funding to individual artists, as well as to galleries showing work in a new context (A Space is the only gallery attempting to grapple with some of these issues); arts councils have a very narrow view of what constitutes

visual art; preponderance of Eurocentric values in both arts councils and in the arts community as a whole.

PRACTICE:
Appropriation of images by white artists.

CURATING:
Decontextualization of work as in *The Spirit Rises* at the Glenbow Museum and the MOMA exhibition on Primitivism; difficulty in getting a certain kind of work into mainstream galleries.

CRITICAL ACCEPTANCE:
Failure on part of critics to recognize non-Eurocentric work, as well as work in the modernist tradition done by non-European artists, e.g., the critical neglect of Black Abstract Expressionist artists in the U.S.

SOLUTIONS:
Formation of networking/support groups like Diasporic African Women's Art (DAWA); A Space providing space and support for shows like *Weapons of Culture* and *Black Wimmin: When and Where We Enter.*

STILL TO BE DONE:
Increased funding;
Better understanding on the part of arts councils, of other cultural languages.

WHERE THEY'RE AT:
REPORTS ON ARTS COUNCILS & ARTS ORGANIZATIONS

Funding by arts councils is often the life blood for many artists: without it many visual artists, for instance, could not practise their art. Accepting that we live in a racist society, we can expect that arts councils, funding bodies, and

professional groups such as the League of Canadian Poets and the Writer's
Union will reflect the racism present in the society at large. It may not be the
aggressive type of racism by commission; it often is the more gentle and,
therefore, more pernicious type of racism by omission such as failure to
appoint to juries individuals and artists representative of non-European
cultures.

The issues facing us when we attempt to analyze critically the workings of arts
councils are complex ones, and ones which are beyond the scope of this
particular exploration; but suffice it to describe them briefly here. As
demonstrated by the information above, there is the issue of the
representative nature of the juries and boards; there is also the issue of
multiculturalism, how it intersects with anti-racist work, and how it works to
muddy the issue of racism and, at times, obscure it. I have always believed
that multiculturalism was concocted, in part, to diffuse the explosive potential
of racism which, at best, has remained an unachieved goal. Finally, but equally
important, is the composition of staff of these bodies— how representative
they are of the society in which we live, which takes us into the area of
affirmative action or, for those who blanch at that expression, employment
equity.

In order to assess where arts councils and professional organizations are
regarding anti-racism and/or affirmative action policies, I sent out the following
brief questionnaire:

1. Does your organization have a clearly articulated policy on anti-racism
and/or affirmative action?
2. If you are a funding organization, does your organization have a clearly
articulated policy on anti-racism and/or affirmative action applicable to your
funding practices?
3. If you have such a policy please send materials documenting that policy and
please furnish examples of how the policy is implemented.
4. If your organization does not have such a policy, do you see a need for

such a policy and have you made any attempts to implement such a policy?

What follows is a synopsis of the replies.

THE CANADA COUNCIL

The Council is included in the federal government's Employment Equity Act and reports annually on their staffing record. I didn't ask about percentages, so no percentages were provided.
There is no affirmative action or anti-racist policy on funding.
Within the context of the Multiculturalism Act, the Council is beginning to examine policies, programmes and practices to make sure they conform to the Act. Native arts have been targeted in the Council's long-range planning exercise.
Specific programmes and/or practices addressing Native arts currently in operation are as follows:

The Northern Canada Jury for Explorations. The jury includes members drawn from Native and Inuit communities from the North;
The Writing and Publication Section accepts applications from eligible publishers publishing in Native languages;
Candidates for Arts Awards writing grants may submit material in their language of origin. External assessments are sought in that language, then submitted to the English or French-language jury;
There is a Native Curatorial Residency in Visual Arts; the jury is composed of Native people.

* The Council needs another $47 million for the arts. If this money is not forthcoming, then there will be continued cuts to programmes and the needed expansion and development of programmes to make them more sensitive to minority groups will certainly not take place. Those arts which are

viewed as "minority"— not truly Canadian— will be the first to go, or will
remain unfunded or underfunded.

** There are no other comparable programmes for any other non-European
cultural groups. For instance, there is no provision made for Black artists
working in a demotic (dialect) English to have their work assessed externally.

DEPARTMENT OF EXTERNAL AFFAIRS:
ARTS PROMOTION DIVISION

There was no response to my questionnaire despite a follow up phone call.
The Arts Promotion Division under their Literature and Publishing
Programme "supports Canadian participation in major international
conferences on literature of importance to Canada." I myself tried to get
support to attend the First International Conference of Caribbean Women
Writers, held in Boston in 1988. I was unsuccessful. My impression was that
such a conference was not considered to be dealing with "literature of
importance to Canada." I protested this approach in a long letter to the
department outlining the importance of Caribbean women writers in Canada,
and their importance to the Caribbean Canadian population.

METRO CULTURAL AFFAIRS (Metropolitan Toronto)

Metro Cultural Affairs appears to be looking both at the composition of its
staff as well as the composition of its resource lists from which their panels
and juries are drawn, with a view to making them more racially and ethnically
representative of the community of Metropolitan Toronto.
In September, 1988, Council passed the following recommendations:

"It is further recommended that the Chief Administrative Officer be
requested to report to Council early in 1989 with a proposal for the

redevelopment of a multicultural policy for service programmes directly operated by the Municipality of Metropolitan Toronto and services purchased, and of the strategy for the implementation of such a policy."

Metro Cultural Affairs comes under these proposals, but changes come slowly in bureaucracies so I do not anticipate any major changes in the near future. I recommended to Metro Cultural Affairs that one of the easiest ways to begin to make changes was to ensure their resource list begin to reflect the diversity of the city in the cultural field.

* The issue of maintaining professional standards was raised at my meeting with the Metro Cultural Affairs representative. My position then and now is that it is a false dichotomy to suggest that professionalism and cultural representation of non-European aesthetics are mutually exclusive. Groups often appear to, and sometimes do lack professionalism because they cannot obtain adequate funding, which in turn makes them appear amateurish. Catch 22!

THE ONTARIO ARTS COUNCIL

The OAC has a clearly articulated personnel policy on non-discrimination. The Council also complies with the Human Rights Code, 1981, and tries to provide "a work environment which is free from racial or sexual harassment." Two new positions which have recently been set up at the Council: Multicultural Coordinator and Native and Folk Arts Associate. Among the duties of the former will be that of developing "a number of additional programme initiatives in the next year specifically addressed to multicultural objectives."
In 1988 the OAC received an additional $30,000 "to assist in funding additional activity or initiatives of a multicultural or folk art nature." Among groups receiving funding from this fund were Emerald City Theatre Company,

Theatre in the Rough, *Tiger Lily,* Imani Theatre Ensemble, Theatre of Change, and the Association of Gospel Music Ministries.

* The OAC *appears* to be broadening its resource list from which it draws jury members so that it draws on all artists from the community.

** The video, *Art Is!,* the OAC's 25th anniversary video which premiered on September 7, 1988, presented an inaccurate picture of the arts in Ontario. There was one brief image of a Black artist and brief clips of Asian members of the symphony. After sitting through this video I felt that the video ought to be renamed *Art Is White!* The video gave no indication of the many, many African, Asian, and Native artists working seriously at their art.

While I welcome the increased funding for Black groups under the multicultural mandate, what concerns me is the real possibility of ghettoizing multiculturalism as Other while "real art" or "true art"— read Eurocentric art— remains at the centre of cultural representation in Ontario.

*** The OAC has had funds from their "new" multicultural budget (from Citizenship and Culture) for the last year. As far as I have been able to ascertain, disbursement of this fund functions as follows. At the officer's discretion, applications are removed from the jury process and reviewed by advisors, picked by the officer, under the terms of a multicultural art defined as providing the initiatives of: linkages, access, and information; bridging mechanisms to overcome language and cultural barriers; new audiences, ensuring that pluralistic art forms are exposed to a wider public.
Final decisions, however, are made at the officer level.

**** The absolute lack of community consultation in defining these initiatives and the "bureauspeak" of the language, seriously jeopardize any commitment the OAC may claim towards instituting a representative multicultural policy. This is appalling.

TORONTO ARTS COUNCIL

The Council adheres to the City of Toronto's Non-Discrimination Policy and
grant applicants and recipients must sign a "declaration of the formal adoption
of a non-discrimination policy as a condition of receipt of a grant."
The Council's staff participates in the City's Equal Opportunity Programme.
"Arts discipline committees, which make recommendations to the board, and
the Toronto Arts Council Nominations Committee are working to ensure
that board and committee membership reflect the racial and ethnic diversity
of the City of Toronto."— Rita Davies, Executive Director.

THE WRITERS' UNION

The Union replied that their eligibility criteria were based entirely on a person
being a Canadian citizen or landed immigrant, with a trade book in print.
Although their letter to me stated that they had enclosed an application form
which set out eligibility criteria, none was enclosed.
The Union also stated that the matter of racism in writing and publishing was
going to be the subject of discussion at their next meeting.

* In 1986, when I was still a member of the Union, I wrote to them
expressing interest in setting up a committee or working on a committee such
as the Rights and Freedoms Committee which would look at racism in
publishing. The Union neither acknowledged my letter nor responded to my
request.

** It is my understanding that in or about 1986 the Union adopted a measure
to increase Union membership among Blacks, Native people and other
minorities. To date nothing has been done about that.

*** In preparation for this piece I approached the Union and requested to

read a debate that had taken place in the Union's newsletter, *Writers'
Confidential*, on the issues of racism and the writer and voice which had arisen
out of The Women's Press situation. I heard nothing further from the Union
until its reply to my questionnaire in which I was told it wasn't possible to give
me access. I do not know if this was, in fact, a decision of the National
Council, or a decision made at the Toronto office. While I respect the Union's
decision in this matter and its reliance on its protocol, I am interested in
knowing whether a decision was ever sought from the National Council
before the Union became involved in The Women's Press dispute. In that
particular instance, on behalf of writers, *none of whom were members of the
Union*, they issued a warning to all Union members not to do business with
The Women's Press until further notice.
If suspension of protocol and rules is possible in a situation that the Union
obviously perceived as having larger significance, surely it is justified when a
writer is seriously interested in looking at the issue or racism in the arts—
particularly writing and publishing— with a view to moving the debate along
the road to a solution. Is the Union genuinely interested in ridding the writing
and publishing world of racism, or merely interested in protecting the turf of
its white middle class membership?

**** I was able to read the debate— through other sources— and it
confirmed my concerns that for the most part Union opinion reveals a
profound lack of concern for the practice of racism in the writing world.

THE LEAGUE OF CANADIAN POETS

The League has not replied to the questionnaire. The Executive Director told
me that the questionnaire had been received and that the President wished
to answer it himself.

What follows are relevant statistics on readings sponsored by the League:

Composition of League:
Men 54% (approx.)
Women 36%
Poets of colour 10%

Readings:
Men 61.5% (approx.)
Women 37%
Poets of colour 1.5%

END NOTES:

1. It is, I believe, no coincidence that Rushton's theories have come to the fore at this point in time in Canada, when racism against African Canadians is on the increase, and when the stand-off between the police and the latter remains at crisis proportions.
2. This manuscript was to be later accepted for publication in England and, irony of ironies, the "new" Women's Press would buy its Canadian rights.
3. ref. to "JOURNAL ENTRIES AGAINST REACTION."
4. African scholars have for years now argued that this was the case; their scholarship has, by and large, been ignored by white mainstream institutions.
5. African scholar Ali Mazrui is the author of several books, including *The Africans*, based on the TV mini-series by the same name.
6. Author of the seminal works *The Cultural Unity of Black Africa* and *The*

African Origin of Civilization.

7. Martin Bernal, *Black Athena*, Rutgers University Press, 1987.

8. John Yau, "Please Wait by the Coatroom," *Arts Magazine*, December, 1988.

9. Moodley in Stanley R. Barrett, *Is God a Racist?*, Toronto: University of Toronto Press, 1988, p. 326.

10. Walter Rodney, *The Grounding with My Brothers*, London: Bogle, L'Overture Publication, 1969, p. 16.

11. Ibid.

12. *New Statesman*, May 27, 1988.

13. Ibid.

14. Ibid.

15. Readers will have noted that when referring to non-European artists, I have, for the most part, particularized them as African, Asian and Native. With the falling into disrepute of the use of the word "Black" as a political concept, this writer can no longer rely on its use in describing all non-Europeans, although the treatment meted out to these groups may essentially be similar. I have, however, in this section used *Black* synonymously with African; if what I describe applies to other non-European groups, they will have to extrapolate from the information provided.

16. For a more detailed analysis of multiculturalism and arts councils, I refer readers to "The Multicultural Whitewash," *FUSE*, Fall, 1987, and elsewhere in this collection.

There Will Be No Peace

There will be no peace.
Fight back, then, with such courage as you have
And every unchivalrous dodge you know of,
Clear in your conscience on this:
Their cause, if they had one, is nothing to them now;
They hate for hate's sake.[1]

WHY DOES IT HAVE ALL THE OVERTONES of the *Last Stand at O.K. Corral* or *High Noon*, where the "good guy cowboy" tells the "bad guy cowboy" he has until noon to get out of town? How life imitates art imitating life imitating... It is now past the hour by some 23 minutes exactly, and I have finally decided to sit and write something— *anything* about this war in the Gulf.

I have been putting it off for some time, although I have, on occasion, been moved to make notes about my responses to the coverage of this "mother of a war." I have put if off because I have been hoping that somehow a resolution would come, and at various times there has been the appearance— various glimmers— that maybe, just maybe, something would give.

So, at the eleventh hour, I have decided to become a witness and to witness; to sit and commit myself, my thoughts and my feelings to paper. This is not an analysis— there are enough of those, some excellent, others mere propaganda. I am interested in witnessing and all that that word implies. We can witness

silently— often a powerful form of witnessing— or we can witness
and testify about our witness.

These writings are but the ordinary words of an ordinary
woman in extraordinary circumstances— they fall somewhere
between witnessing and testifying on this screen— this little
marvel of technology that pilots flying bombing missions over
Iraq are also using.

How implicated we all are in this enterprise— *our* use of the
computer with its screen and image apparently peaceful, *theirs*
warlike. But surely we are contaminated by the uses of the
technology— the wonder-chip technology that we, in the West,
have embraced so eagerly— never mind the ill effects on the eyes
and health of those making these little machines somewhere else
in the "Third World," or is it the non-world as far as the U.S.
and other so-called Western democracies are concerned?

Technology— the god that rules the world with a savage
unforgivingness, putting to shame any Old Testament god.
Technology that inspires hubris in its makers and believers who,
believing, bomb indiscriminately. They believed they could
bomb Viet Nam out of existence; they found instead a poor
"Third World" country that defied that technology, eventually
causing the most technologically advanced country in this world,
albeit "with one hand tied behind its back," to back down. And
back off! Technology had reckoned without the human spirit.
Emotive, meaningless words perhaps— the human spirit— but
aren't we just machines, meaningless machines without it?

Once again technology goes to war— this time with super
weapons, Nintendo style, to do battle with the human spirit.
Once again the super-power states have failed to factor in the
human spirit, the will— the Iraqi will against American technol-

ogy. The human spirit? Saddam Hussein? Isn't he just a barbarian deserving of a country filled with other barbarians— lacking such qualities as the human spirit?

Saddam, the barbarian; Saddam, the Arab Hitler; Saddam, the mad man. And, of course, the unspoken corollary: Bush the civilized; Bush, the American Churchill; Bush, the sane, the rational. But isn't it just that one evil now faces another and we, the spectators, are expected to choose the lesser of the two? And aren't we seeing the coming to fruition of rationality— the madness, the irrationality, if you will, of rationality taken to its logical and radical extreme in the weapons of technology? That terrible craziness which has *always* been at the heart of Western society— I hesitate to use the word civilization— is now full blown, and there is a collective madness afoot, stoked and nursed carefully by the "leaders" of the coalition and its handmaidens, the media. Madness b(e)aring the face of rationality. Those of us carrying black skins have always known this madness, our histories scored by its effects, which towards us has taken the form of white supremacy. It comes as no surprise— it is disturbingly familiar, yet surprising all the same.

Saddam Hussein has abused his power; he has abused his people, he is Machiavellian but but... Let him who is without sin cast the first stone. Others have done what he has done. And worse. Even those now throwing the biggest stones have thrown yet bigger ones at small nations— Grenada, Nicaragua, and Panama to name but three. So clearly what is at stake here is not that Saddam is a bad boy and has to be punished. The stakes are higher— much higher: the industrially developed North against the industrially deprived South; rich nations against poor; white against Black; the war to secure raw materials for the

great consuming maw of the capitalist machine. We must! Make
no mistake about it, the U.S. will do similarly again— if and when
the need for other raw materials arises.

To what use will the 25% of oil Kuwait supplies the West
be put? To make more weapons? To produce more goods the
West doesn't need; to pollute the atmosphere and environment
further? Surely, countries that have been able to devise the
dazzling array of war technology could have advanced, by this
time, more innovative ways of trapping pre-existing energy
sources? Solar power, for instance. Why hasn't this happened?
And why the overwhelming development of the technology of
death?—

the eagle comes home
to roost— tearing
its breast— eating
its young
the eagle comes home

I see Saddam Hussein as an agent of history— unwittingly
sacrificing his country to reveal, not only the inherent inequities
and immoralities that pass for international law and politics, but
also the intentions of the most militarily powerful country in the
world, the United States. The new world order of which Bush
speaks will be even more militantly and militarily aggressive and
economically exploitative. As is often the case, we seldom have
an opportunity to choose our agents, but accept them we must,
garbed in all their blood and gore even while we grieve the
innocent civilians— too often women and children— killed and
maimed as a consequence of their actions.

Saddam, Bush, Assiz, Mulroney, Clark— who *are* these
men— who *are* these men? Talking rationally of death, mayhem
and murder— your death, my death— so easy, so easy, using
language to hide the dying; the flippant tone, the stern words—
who *are* these men? "A sentence uttered makes a world ap-
pear/where all things happen as it says they do;/we doubt the
speaker, not the tongue we hear:/words have no word for words
that are not true."[1] So writes Auden playing with time then. And
now. Words have no words for words that are not true, and we
are left bereft of language except body bags, collateral damage,
KIA's and evacuating ordinances— words have no words for
words! Who *are* these men? Where are the women? Would we
make a difference? And how? Consider Mrs. Thatcher— we have
been spared her chauvinistic vitriol, but we can all write her
script.

If, however, we wanted any proof about who controls the
bottom line, where the buck stops, and who decides who lives
and who dies, we have had it. In living colour every night in our
living rooms. Men. Men. And more. Men. All men— sometimes
white, sometimes black, sometimes brown, but always. Men.
Who erect tombs to the unknown soldier.

"See the Unknown Soldier known/to all of us. A woman
cradles/his head with her tears— /the Unknown Mother, for
whom/there have been no graves, no medals,/no cenotaphs,
except those of her sons/shows her bloodied face, bares
her/teeth, aspirates the Word and makes it flesh." In 1983 I
wrote that, and still the Unknown Mother weeps for her sons
and daughters. Nine months and a universe of love— that's how
long it takes us to ripen life to living inside us— "It takes about
eighteen months for one/To ripen into a skeleton,"[1] not to "be

washed, folded, packed, in a small/Niche hollowed out of the cemetery wall,"[1] but to be heat dried and blown by winds of the desert storm.

"Words have no words for words that are not true," hiding the body dying behind the words. They, the harbingers of death, have hidden death from us behind the words— as the doctor listens to my heart

takes my pulse
palpates the skin stretched
taut over guts
bones— so frail
pokes his hands in me
so fragile
this body human
boosting itself with
missiles and bombs
broken across the world
and Patriots proving
the inherent optimism of stocks
have risen to
march to death
lurking in the spill of guts
the stench of shit
the blood giving red its
meaning and
words words and more words—
the first casualty of war.

And today a Soviet space craft travelling at god knows how many miles per hour crashes to earth, while the skies of Baghdad light up with a thousand points of light. They have mined the world with a thousand points of evil while weapons experts convert death to numbers and tonnage and "Truth, is convertible to kilowatts..."[1]

This collective madness with the face of rationality that makes it all the more unnerving. And along with this, the helplessness that so very many of us have felt— consigned to the ultimate role of consumer— consumers of death by numbers, death by language, death by graphics. And we can do nothing— our role but to consume the lies. And the death.

"Evil incarnate"— emotive words, words having biblical resonances, and yet whenever I hear these men speak of death— these are the words that come to mind. Evil incarnate. Evil made flesh; evil in the body. What is this evil? Merely an absence of good? Or is it an active force for ill? I think it the latter. And I have seen the face of evil couched in words of a kinder, gentler demon. Who arrogantly raises the possibility of toppling the King of Jordan because he dared oppose the United States.

These are the ordinary and not so ordinary words of an ordinary woman in extraordinary circumstances, facing the utter helplessness in the face of evil. Made flesh.

Why am I not surprised at the change in aims? I always knew that the aim was to get rid of Saddam. I am far from the circles and squares of powers, and yet I know. And how to explain this mass collective acquiescence? Mass murder. Words that have come to resonate with the plight of the Jews in World War II. History was profoundly implicated in that. It is probably a marker of both imperialist racism and a happy childhood as an African Caribbean child, that my introduction to evil was that perpetrated on the Jews in effort of their attempted obliteration. But now we stand by— helpless— and witness mass murder being

committed by weapons of mass destruction, by the most powerful country in the world. And silent.

To be silent in the face of torture is to do good, *and* to accept
pain. After release, breaking the silence is also to do good; to be
silent then is to collude with one's silencers. We have been
silenced, but we must not accept this silence. How do we resist
the silencing?

By witnessing.

In conversation with a friend recently, we both, with some
surprise, agreed that political work as much as religious life
demanded faith; we often have to continue to struggle for
political goals in the face of great opposition, when all appears
to be contrary to what we want to have happen. Faith— the
substance of things hoped for and the evidence of things not
seen is one definition, albeit Biblical. The evidence of things not
seen— the words of the spiritual "How long, Lord, how long?"
come to mind, and the profound condemnation of so many,
whose voices are not heard. On prime time. This is the only
evidence yet of a new world whose order lies in justice and
equality.

As far as the substance of things hoped for— it is my hope
that the strategic and historical role of Saddam Hussein points
not only to the bleak issues outlined above, but also to an
eventual coming together by countries of the South— Africa,
Asia, Latin America and the Caribbean— in some sort of
economic union. Until then, which I suspect will be a long time
coming, these writings, in the words of Bob Marley, are "my
songs of freedom/cause all I ever had— [were] redemption songs,
redemption songs."

Peace without justice, Martin Luther King Jr. said, was not
peace, and so even if there were "peace" tomorrow, without the

resolution of deep-seated issues of justice in that part of the world, there will be other Saddams. There *will be* no peace.

END NOTE:

1. Unless otherwise identified, all quotations are from Auden's *Collected Works*.

Letter: July, 1990

Conversations Across Borders

Yo Jan!

If anyone had told me, on coming to Banff, that the person I was most likely to have hard political conversation and dialogue with was a white, American woman from San Diego, I would have said "no way." And I'm not sure why I'm surprised— maybe I let labels get in the way. On thinking about your being gay and the experiences you've shared with me, I see reasons why we would understand each other's experiences and understand how difficult it is to resist becoming what the dominant culture defines you as— nigger, fag, or dyke.

Over the last few weeks here I have heard myself raising the issue of the absence of Native people from the residency on border cultures and, at the last meeting, I explained why it was important for me to address that question. I am going to try to again, but before going any further I do want to say that what I have observed is that Native people are not exactly absent from Banff; in fact, their presence increases commensurately the lower down the staff hierarchy you go. I have noticed quite a few among the staff that clean the rooms, and to complicate matters immediately, I've also noticed that the presence of Francophones increases among the lower ranks.

Let me be up front and straight: the absence of Native artists in the border culture residency is, in my opinion, a form of silencing of the Native voice in Canadian cultural practice, as well as a reflection of that silencing. To continue being up front and straight, I recognize that the expression of my concern comes too late. I had noticed this absence when I received the list of participants; the principled thing to have done then was to have raised it as an issue and taken some action on the matter.

We are all implicated in this silencing whether or not we agree with it— I don't believe anyone in our group does— just as we are implicated— whether we like it or not— in certain inequities in this world. By virtue of our relatively privileged existences here in the West *all* our hands are soiled— the coffee we drink; the cheap clothes we wear; the computers we use are but three simple examples of this privilege which has been bought at the expense of others. The problem is that no matter how much we want to, we can do little about this form of exploitation. To stop drinking coffee, wearing cheap clothes, or using computers made by the exploited labour of women somewhere in the Third World, in no way means that those exploited women or men will be guaranteed a better life or any life at all. There is always another consumer out there to buy these products. I believe, however, what we must do, those of us who understand the price others pay for our often undesired privilege, is position ourselves or use our position here in the belly of the whale— *in* the First World, to critique and challenge the assumptions by which the Western world fuels itself; we must prevent the miasma of smug I'm-O.K.-rhetoric from spreading more than it has already spread. This is fundamentally where my concern about the absence of the Native presence is coming from.

If I understand that the ideology of white supremacy which

decimated the aboriginal peoples in Canada and the U.S., not to mention the Caribbean, Central and South America, was the same which enslaved my people in Africa and the Caribbean, and attempted to obliterate our culture; if I understand that white supremacy as practised here in Canada against the Native people, set the stage for the treatment of Black immigrants to this country; if I understand how white supremacy continues to wreak havoc today against the Native peoples of Canada, how can I be silent about their absence. Their Silence (as in the sense I use it in *Looking for Livingstone*) has a grammar, and a poetics; can be parsed, and quantified, and has spoken volumes to me at this site— one of the largest and most powerful site specific installations of Eurocentric culture outside Europe.

I cannot presume to speak on behalf of Native artists and will not. I only have the facts. Consider the high rates of unemployment, and the high incidence of infant mortality, wife and child abuse, and alcoholism among the Native communities; consider also the fact that not too long ago a young Native child burnt to death on a reserve in this part of the country, because the fire department refused to come to the reserve— they claimed the reserve hadn't paid their fees; consider the fact that a recent inquest into the murder of a young Native woman by white men many years ago revealed that many people, including police officers, knew who was implicated in the murder and did nothing about it for several years. Consider, finally, a recent report from a one-man commission of inquiry into the justice system and the wrongful incarceration for murder of a young Mic Mac, Donald Marshall, in Nova Scotia, which stated that there were two systems of justice operating in that province— one for whites and one for Natives. Nova Scotia is not unique in Canada, Jan— merely typical. I could go on and ask you to consider also the forced sterilization of Native women. I could go on, but I won't.

What I will do, however, is call attention and describe the silence I feel created by the omission of the Native tradition from a gathering of outstanding artists around the concept and idea of borders. For me to say nothing, which is not the same as being silent, would be to collude in that silencing, which would make me even more derelict in my responsibility as a writer, particularly since I believe that the social context within which one practises one's art is as important as, in some instances more than, the skill involved.

I acknowledge that the creation of a space in an institution such as this, to allow issues and questions like these to be raised is something of a breakthrough, or, to be more accurate, a hairline fracture, in the massive structure of Eurocentric culture. Our gratefulness for this ought not, however, to work to silence us about very grave issues such as those Rasheed Areen[1] (your quotation) talks about. I believe we have determined the source of domination at the Banff Centre— Eurocentric culture and all its assumptions, even when disguised in po.mo. (post modernist) rhetoric— and we would not be amiss in concluding that the effect of the "power relations" to use Areen's phrase, in terms of "production, recognition and validation" works to silence Native artists within this context.

Inertia is a powerful force and postmodern capitalism would very much prefer us to accept its assumptions unquestioningly, consume a bit more and leave everything to Big Daddy or Maggie. After all, who would want to disturb the contemplation of nature, or sully this paradise, albeit bureaucratic and artificial, with crass thoughts about racism— and in Canada at that? Laughing and talking about Mount Rundle appears a far more rewarding activity. And doesn't "great art" get created in environments like this, where the artist can go on a hike and commune with nature? Romanticism is alive and well. In Banff! Because before you know it, you have suspended your critique forged in what is essentially a hostile, racist and sexist environment, and you forget to question how and where a place like Banff fits in the cultural practice of Canada.

While the receptivity– or lack thereof– of a Eurocentric institution to non-Europeans is an important issue, we cannot, however, let the apparent impenetrability of the Banff Centre prevent us from asking pertinent questions about the absence of Native artists from the Border Culture Residency, where they would appear to fit most naturally. One of the markers of oppressed groups is the fact that their members have had to learn how to cross borders and boundaries; functioning in a white world or work place and then returning "home" to the ghetto or to the family, is all of a piece with Black life. I am convinced that Native people have been making similar journeys across boundaries of race and culture to earn a living or merely to survive, from the time the European landed on these shores. So the argument which has been made, that the Banff Centre *first* has to become receptive and sensitive to Native artists *before* they can be invited, is to wait for hell to freeze over.

Furthermore, if no one invites them, who will speak on their behalf; who will challenge the racist practices? Neither is it sufficient that a Native artist will be coming to talk to the artists in the residency. The issue belongs *inside* the residency. It is only when shifts in power are made at the level of curating, for instance, that any possibility of true change is possible. I would argue that it is now fairly received opinion that women ought to be in charge of events that relate to them specifically. I have found, however, that when it comes to race, the same understanding and acceptance of this principle doesn't exist.

I keep coming back to responsibility and the practice of art—if we claim certain privileges and rights as artists (Do we? The existence of the Banff Centre certainly suggests that we do), and if we accept that just by virtue of where we live, the language we speak, the education we've had, we *are* privileged, then we must ask ourselves what the concomitant responsibilities are. And in this setting one of my responsibilities is to question, question and question further. Is the absence of Native artists from the residency and the silence about the issue but another manifestation of Canada refusing to deal with its own domestic racism, but only too happy to focus on racism practised by its big bad neighbour to the south— the United States of America? What types of borders does the present Canadian fascination and flirtation with multiculturalism elide and what sorts of borders does it erect? How do multicultural organizations in Canada, such as arts councils, all of which manifest forms of systemic racism, deal with issues of race and the borders between races, particularly when certain races and therefore their cultural practices, are considered to be superior?

Racism is a growth industry in today's world and, like the multinational, knows no boundaries. Hearing about cross-border racism and imperialism between the U.S. and Mexico ought naturally to lead to questions of cross "border" racism and imperialism here in Canada. Starting with the Native issue. But the response has been a general anti-Americanism. And silence. Neither of which is going to lead to fruitful dialogue. Both of which work to leave things as they are. CONSIDER INSTEAD THE LANDSCAPE! AND THE ELK AND THE MOUNTAINS!

For many artists from less materially privileged countries, the material plenitude offered by Banff is a welcome change, and I am happy that Canada, through Banff, has provided an opportunity for me to meet artists like Magda and Jose and Leonora and Angel. My responsibility to them as a Black writer in Canada is to let them know that there are Third World realities right here in this First World country, Canada; that Banff is an aberration in the cultural practice of African, Asian and Native artists in Canada. Artists from these communities have been engaged in a protracted struggle to resist appropriation of their cultures; to eradicate racism in funding and cultural practices such as book publishing and curating, and to develop strategies that ensure cultural institutions treat them and their work with respect.

I wish them to know the contempt which the literary establishment of this country has for Black writers like myself, as manifested recently by George Bowering, one of the preeminent members of this establishment, writing and publishing in the *Globe and Mail* that he had read my poetry and was very surprised to see that I was a good poet! I want them to know that racism is alive and kicking shit all across this country; that in Toronto, for instance, four Black people have been shot by the police in the last two years, in situations that didn't warrant those shootings; that similar shootings have taken place in Montreal; not to mention the long history of racism in Nova Scotia against the oldest Black population in this country—Blacks who came to Canada from the U.S. as Loyalists. (In exchange for their loyalty to the Crown, Black Loyalists were promised land and other benefits. Those promises were never kept.) I could go on about studies showing that Blacks are three times as unlikely as whites to get jobs; but I won't.

As I have been writing this, Jan, I have been asking myself

whether my concern with the Native issue is merely a displace-
ment of my concern with issues having to do with Black people—
but no— I do believe profoundly that we can't build our new
realities on the oppression of others, and equality, dignity and
respect gained at the expense of someone else's respect and
dignity is a chimaera. And I have just turned on the radio and
heard something that confirms for me that the Native issue is
pre-eminent in this country. The Nova Scotian government has
just awarded Donald Marshall, whom I mentioned above, a
substantial settlement for the 11 years he spent in jail for a
murder he did not commit. I have also tuned in to the end of a
phone-in show on the Meech Lake Accord with Elijah Harper,
the Native MP who did a Rosa Parks on Meech Lake. In response
to a caller who said that Natives were promised that once the
Quebec issue was settled the Native issue would be "high on the
agenda"— yes, his words, Harper said that *for several centuries*
they had been "promised" certain things, and those promises
had never been kept.

Wherever he strayed outside Europe, the European was met
with generosity; he has always returned this by speaking with
forked tongue and for once he's been called on it. It sometimes
only takes one honest man or woman, eh! It's not that I don't
accept that the French have been screwed and ROYALLY, and
they ought to be able to preserve their culture and language, and
have their own country, if that is what they want, but again to
position myself as I did at the beginning, it seems to me that
what we have is two European peoples arguing over land that
was stolen in the first place. And surely we've got to deal with
that initial theft and compensation for it, *before* we deal with
anything else. And speaking of Native people and reserves and
Canada— how many Canadians know or care to know that the

South Africans got their ideas for Bantustans and homelands from Canadian reserves! A group of South Africans visited Canada to look at how the system of reserves worked— the year escapes me— and returned home and set up the homelands! Mandela ought to have met with the Native chiefs in Alberta— the links are deeper than many of us think.

What more can I say? What does all of this have to do with art? Everything. And nothing. Everything in the sense that these are facts against which (in both senses) I write. Nothing— in the sense that for many of us, to write or practise our art requires a supreme act of belief in ourselves, in the face of a system and culture that conspires to silence us, to make us believe that we are nothing. And in believing in ourselves we have to assign the value of zero (= nothing) to those other beliefs. In your other quotation by Areen, he talks of the European practice of documenting and studying the cultures of those to whom they ascribe the status of Other. I believe that we too are engaged in a similar documentation and study. But of European cultural practices, from an entirely different perspective and with an entirely different aim. Our correspondence is an important part of this documentation, since Banff is a significant marker of cultural practice here in Canada. We ought to put our writings— our markings— into the box that the Border Culture residents have committed themselves to putting together. When Banff changes, as it most certainly will, it will be an important record, from our perspective, of what it was all about. For too damn long we have had to read their records on us. It is about time they begin to read our records on them.

All the best in your work and my love,
Nourbese.

P.S. Jan—

How difficult it is to believe in ourselves— not to dismiss our dreams as merely rant. We are only a minority in this country, after all. The question is how did certain groups get to be a minority— the Natives, genocide; the Blacks, racism. I'm writing this postscript because since writing the letter I've been walking around the campus and hearing voices. The two people whom I identified in "Who's Listening"[2]— the Oxford-educated English man, John, and the wizened old Black woman, Abiswa. He tells me that I'm full of shit— that this place is built on excellence and that colour and race are immaterial. He tells me to pick up the brochure on the summer festival and read the President's welcome— "artists... who have come here to stretch their imaginations and their skills into a tautness as tough as iron and supple as leather." He shows me the opera rehearsal studio, points out the two Black performers— asks me what more I want and tells me that what people said about me was true— "You're a troublemaker!" And all I want is to crawl away and cry and forget it all, because I didn't want to see any of this when I came here— I came only to write, I told myself— only to write, to escape politics and politicking.

The image that comes to mind strangely enough is the temptation of Jesus in the desert— where the devil offers him cities and principalities, if he would just admit that he, the devil, was the head honcho. In my case this cultured urbane Oxonian wants my silence and shows me the Banff Centre as proof that he is the boss and my silence will confirm it. Through my tears, I notice, Abiswa, the little old lady laughing and laughing, then she starts twirling and spinning as she sings a low, melodious tune in a language I don't recognize. When she's done she calls me over and says— "Chile, there was many a day during slavery

time when we did wish we could tell others who were lucky
enough to stay back home in Africa, what was happening to us—
the drums didn't travel that far across the ocean. All you have
to do is tell it like it is, so we remembering. You see how he
gone— like the devil, he don't like hear the truth." I laugh and
look around and John has disappeared. So maybe, Jan, I was
right after all about documenting and recording and telling it
like it is— despite the consequences. Stresses and problems there
have been in the residency— we are all aware of them, but nothing
that is worthwhile gets born or created easily, and a space has
been created for debate, dialogue and conversation. What we
have to do is make the space larger and wider so our voices— *all*
our voices can be heard. And this is happening through vehicles
like Angel's paper, the radio station and this correspondence. I
hope you can continue the debate with the other residents— they
are a fine group! Once again, my love to you and all the others.

From correspondence between M. Nourbese Philip and Jan Schaefer at the
1990 Border Culture Workshop held at Banff, Alberta, and published in the
Border Cultures newsletter.

END NOTES:

1. Rasheed Areen, "From Primitivism to Ethnic Arts," Third Text, Vol. 1,
Autumn, 1987.
2. See "Who's Listening? artists, audiences & language," elsewhere in this
collection.

The Disappearing Debate

Or, how the discussion of racism has been taken over by the censorship issue

ARGUMENT BY THE WHITE MIDDLE CLASS, for the white middle class, about the white middle class. Such was the long-winded, rather tedious debate that took place in last winter's newsletters of the Writers' Union, relating to issues of censorship and the writer and voice. This debate had been sparked by the rejection of three short stories by The Women's Press for an anthology of short fiction, *Imagining Women*, on the grounds that the writers in question, all white, had drawn on and used the voices of characters from cultures and races other than their own. The Press also took issue with the use, by one of the writers, of magic realism, a style pioneered in Latin America. According to the Press, these practices constituted racism. To buttress this position, the Press issued policy guidelines stating that it would "avoid publishing manuscripts in which the protagonist's experience in the world, by virtue of race or ethnicity, is substantially removed from that of the writer."

As often happens around issues such as these, the debate quickly assumed a dichotomous nature with the pro-censorship forces arrayed against the anti-censorship hordes. Racism was the issue that detonated the explosion at The Women's Press; to the exclusion of any other, censorship became the issue that has monopolized the media's attention. Censorship of white writers; censorship of the imagination; censorship by publishers. Censorship in all its myriad forms became, in fact, *the* privileged discourse.

The quantum leap from racism to censorship is neither random nor unexpected, since the issue of censorship is central to the dominant cultures of liberal democracies like Canada. In these cultures, censorship becomes a significant and talismanic cultural icon around which all debates about the "individual freedom of *man*" swirl. It is the cultural and political barometer which these societies use to measure their freedoms. Censorship is as important to the state intent on imposing it as it is to those who are equally committed to opposing it.

Since writers and artists are, by and large, the ones who express the cultural ideas of their age, their individual and collective roles are crucial to the process that assigns significance to ideas such as censorship. Western liberal democracies, in fact, usually grade their relative freedoms and those of other countries according to the freedoms allowed these self-appointed purveyors of cultural representation. In turn, the latter come to share, in no small way, in the rewards of the system.

Historically, racism has never been assigned a central place in the West. As an issue it has remained remarkably absent from debates on the economy, society or polity; racism, in fact, has never been as privileged a discourse as censorship. In more recent years, however, we have seen the privileging of certain types of racism— such as anti-Semitism— over others: one can easily gauge the degree of privileging by the nature and frequency of media attention, or by government activity on the matter.

Racism against Africans, however, remains a relatively unimportant issue, except in those instances when the latter are perceived as potential or real disruptors of the social fabric. One very effective way of ensuring that this type of racism remains marginal to the dominant culture is to have another issue that is more privileged, such as censorship or freedom of speech. Two recent examples of the privileging of censorship and freedom of speech over issues of race arose from the public lecture at the University of Toronto in 1987 by Glen Babb, the South African consul, and the much-publicized theories of racial superiority by University of Western Ontario professor Philippe Rushton.

In the latter case, despite public outcry and opposition from students, despite widespread reports of his shoddy scholarship, and despite his recommendations that governments act on his findings, Rushton has been allowed to keep his position at the university and to continue teaching. All in the name of freedom of speech.

Furthermore, on those occasions when racism against Blacks does assume a more public profile, as happened in the last few months in Toronto after the shooting of a Black adolescent, it usually occurs in an aberrational context. Racism is thereby reduced to the level of the personal, and presented as a rare form of disease which, if treated appropriately— usually with a task force— will quickly disappear. There is a profound failure, if not a refusal, to understand how thoroughly racism informs all aspects of society.

At the heart of this attitude lies a paradox: the ideology and practice of racism has as old a tradition as that of the "rights of man." While John Locke argued for the freedom of man, he had no intellectual difficulty accepting that these freedoms could not and should not extend to African slaves. The ideological frame-

work of Western democracies, erected upon the belief in freedom
of the individual, is supported as much by this ideology (and its
offshoots), as by that of racism. However, one discourse, censorship, becomes privileged; the other, racism, is silenced. To insist
on its lesser status, thereby excluding it from the dominant forms
and fora of discussion, becomes one of the most effective ways
of perpetuating racism. To do so is, in fact, profoundly racist.

WOMAN AS OTHER CONSTITUTES one of the building blocks of the
patriarchy; Black as Other one of the building blocks of white
supremacist ideologies. The white, male author has never
flinched from representing women or Blacks in his writing,
misogynist and/or racist point of view and all. While many of
the classified "great works of literature" have been novelistic
studies of women by men— *Anna Karenina*, *Madame Bovary* and
Tess of the D'Urbervilles, to name but three, and while there have
always been significant literary sorties into "exotic" cultures by
writers— Kipling, Conrad and Forster come to mind— a quick
survey of English literature reveals that works written from the
point of view of the Other, Black, female or even working class,
have not comprised a major part of that literature. In that respect,
contemporary literature differs not at all.

   The vociferousness, therefore, of the defence of this right—
to write from the point of view of the Other— as we have
witnessed it recently, is clearly disproportionate to the actual
exercise of that right. Is it merely that this right is all of a piece
with the rights accruing to a writer living and writing in a liberal
democracy? Or, does the impulse for the unquestioning defence
of this right lie elsewhere?

   Sara Maitland, the English novelist, writes that "Whether
men can do women's stories is another question, one that

feminist literary discourse asks often; but it is certain that the oppressed develop insights about their oppressors to a greater degree than the other way about because they need them in order to survive."[1] In virtually every sphere of life, women have had to learn what men want and don't want; what turns them on and what doesn't. Black people, in the course of their individual and collective history of labour, have been privy to what no outsider ought to be in another's life. As cleaners, servants, and domestics, Blacks have known when or whether the white master was or wasn't fucking his wife, or anyone else for that matter. Black women have suckled their white charges and, in many instances, provided the latter with emotional nourishment that, through exploitative economic practices, they have been unable to provide their own children. Consider, for example, the many many foreign nannies caring for the children of white Canadians, while their own children remain at home in the Caribbean or the Philippines. As in the case of women, which Maitland so well identifies, to ensure their survival, Blacks have had to know what angry white people look like, and how to recognize when the latter were happy and when not. And today the media, for the most part in flagrant contempt for all but the dominant culture, continue to teach Blacks how their erstwhile masters look as they go about their lives.

It borders on the trite and hackneyed to say that writers tend to draw on what they know best as raw material for their work. "Write what you know" is one of the most consistent pieces of advice given to young writers. One would, therefore, assume that when writers from traditionally oppressed groups begin to come to voice publicly, knowing almost as much about their oppressors as they do about their own lives, they would write about their oppressors— at least as much as they write about themselves.

Blacks about whites; the working class about the middle and upper classes; women about men. They have good reason to do so: they have, by their labour, earned the vision of the insider.

The paradox, however, is that once an oppressed group is finally able to attain the means of making its voice heard— voicing its many silences— it is far less concerned in rendering audible the voice of its oppressors, and infinitely more interested in (and committed to) making public their own reality and their own lives. The explosion in feminist publishing, for instance, has resulted in women writing and publishing their own stories, *about* themselves and *for* themselves. Men have not been entirely absent from these works, but neither has there been a demonstrated eagerness to write from the point of view of men. And so too for Blacks. What Black writers have wanted to voice is not the voice and experiences of the white person, but the reality of Black people, *from the point of view* of Black people. Given the ubiquitous nature of racism, whites or their systems of domination must perforce figure, to a lesser or greater degree, in these works: their point of view will, however, not be privileged.

This paradox ought to give us pause, if nothing else, to wonder why the *ability* to use the voice of the Other, as we have come to know it in literature and art, has for the most part realized itself in the oppressor using the voice of the oppressed, and not the other way around. It is an ability that is first engendered, then supported by the interlocking and exploitative practices of capitalism, racism, and sexism. And, linked as it is to privilege of one sort or another— race, gender, or class, or all three— it is an ability which serves that privilege. It is, in fact, that very privilege that is the enabling factor in the transformation of what is essentially an exercise of power into a right. That right in turn becomes enshrined and privileged in the ideology servicing the society in general.

The "right" to use the voice of the Other has, however, been bought at great price— the silencing of the Other; it is, in fact, neatly posited on that very silence. It is also a right that exists without an accompanying obligation, and as such, can only lead to abuse.

The ability to use the voice of the Other; the "right" to use the voice of the Other. In the trite words of the popular song about love and marriage: "You can't have one without the other." To those who would argue that in a democracy everyone has the right to write from any point of view, I would contend that for far too long certain groups have not had access to any of the resources which enable writing of *any* sort to take place, let alone writing from a particular point of view. Education, financial resources, belief in the validity of one's experiences and reality, whether working class, female or Black: these are all necessary to the production of writing. They are also essential factors in the expression of one's ability to write. The exploitative practices of capitalist economies have, in fact, deprived these groups of the ability to express themselves through writing and publishing. Without that ability, the right to write from *any* point of view is meaningless. It goes without saying that the ability to write without the right is equally meaningless.

ALL OF THIS APPEARS MORE THAN REASON enough to prohibit white writers writing from the point of view of persons from other cultures or races. The emotion— anger at the injustices that flow from racism— is entirely understandable. However, despite the reckless exercise of privilege on the part of white writers, I believe such a proscription to be very flawed and entirely ill-advised. My reasons for this position are as follows: firstly, such a rule or proscription is essentially unenforceable (unless, of course, one is the late Ayatollah) and for that reason should never be made. Secondly, prohibiting such activity alters not one iota of that invisible and sticky web of systemic or structural racism. If all the white writers interested in this type of writing were voluntarily to swear off writing from the point of view of persons from other races and/or cultures, it would not ensure that writers from those cultures or races would get published any more easily, or at all. For that to happen, changes have to be made at other levels and in other areas such as publishing, reviewing, distribution, library acquisitions, and educational curricula. Thirdly, and, to my mind, most importantly, for those who unquestioningly clasp the rights of the individual writer most dearly to their breasts, such a proscription provides a ready-made issue to sink their anti-censorship teeth into. Such a proscription becomes, in fact, a giant red herring dragged across the brutally cut path of racism.

As the fallout from The Women's Press debacle so clearly showed, all available energy in the writing community went into discussing, arguing and debating whether white women writers, or white writers in general, ought or ought not to be using the voice of the Other. There was no discussion about how to enable more Black women to get into print, or how to help those small publishing houses committed to publishing work by Black authors, or any attention paid to the many tasks that must be undertaken to make the writing and publishing world truly non-racist.

Funding, publishing, distribution, critical reception— racism manifests itself in all these areas. For the Black writer the problem is hydra-headed; its effect as multi-faceted as profound.

If, as the late critic Raymond Williams argued, "no work is in any full practical sense produced until it is also received," then much of the writing by Black writers in Canada fails to be fully produced. "Burning books," the Russian poet Joseph Brodsky writes, is "after all... just a gesture; not publishing them is a falsification of time... precisely the goal of the system," intent on issuing "its own version of the future."[2] This "falsification of time" which results from the failure to publish writers is as characteristic of the dominant culture in Canada as in the Soviet Union. In both cases, the state's intention is to "issue its own version of the future." And the Canadian version will, if possible, omit the contributions of Blacks and other non-dominant groups.

It is not that the question of the individual privilege of the white writer is entirely unimportant. That privilege is heavily implicated in the ideology of racism, white supremacy and their practices. The weight of racism in the writing world, however, does not reside with the individual white writer, but in the network of institutions and organizations that reinforce each other in the articulation of systemic racism. The writer is but a cog in that system. It is, perhaps, typical of a liberal democracy that racism in the writing and publishing world would be reduced to the individual writer sitting before her word processor, with only the imagination for company.

The imagination is free! Long live the imagination! One could hear the cry echoing around Canada as the controversy concerning the writer and voice rippled out across the country. Many writers saw the suggestion that they merely consider their social and political responsibility in selecting subject matter as an attempt to control that great storehouse of the writer: the imagination. One writer argued publicly that when she sat at her desk, her imagination took over and she had no choice but to go with it. Are we to conclude, therefore, that there are no mediating actions between what the writer imagines and what eventually appears on the printed page? Are we, as writers, all engaged in some form of literary automatism? While acknowledging that surrealist writers have indulged in automatic writing, the product of their writing was not intended to be realist fiction. The mandate of surrealism, if writing can ever be said to have a mandate, was to challenge what had, until then, been the art traditions of the Western world.

The imagination, I maintain, is both free and unfree. Free in that it can wander wheresoever it wishes; unfree in that it is profoundly affected and shaped by the societies in which we live. Traditionally, the unfettered nature of the imagination has done very little to affect the essentially negative portrayal of women by men in the arts. By and large, this portrayal has conformed closely to patriarchal visions of women. It required, in fact, a feminist reform movement to ensure the more realistic and positive images of women with which we are becoming increasingly familiar.

To state the obvious, in a racist, sexist and classist society, the imagination, if left unexamined, can and does serve the ruling ideas of the time. Only when we understand how belief in the untrammelled nature of the imagination is a part of the dominant culture can we, as Elizam Escobar[3] suggests, begin to use the imagination as a weapon. The danger with writers carrying their unfettered imaginations into another culture— particularly one like the Native Canadian culture which theirs has oppressed and exploited— is that without careful thought, they are likely to perpetuate stereotypical and one-dimensional views of this culture.

Regarding the issue of whether a white writer should use a style pioneered in a Third World country, there is again the problem of unenforceability. There is, however, a more serious error in this approach. The assumption behind the proscription is that because the style in question— magic realism— was pioneered in Latin America, it must, therefore, be entirely a product of that part of the world. Yet much of Latin American culture, particularly that of the middle and upper classes, has traditionally drawn heavily on European culture; the main articulators and purveyors of this style within Latin America— white males for the most part— are products of European learning and tradition. One could further argue that magic realism is as much an heir to European traditions of surrealism, for instance, as to the Latin American sensibility and mindscape. Does that make it a Third World or First World style? Would it be acceptable, then, to use a European style, but not a European style one step removed?

All of this is not to deny that magic realism, as we have come to know it, is inextricably bound up with Latin America and its unique realities. But the proscription and its underlying (and unarticulated) assumptions reveal how little understanding there truly is of the complex nature of these societies and their histories. Latin America plays the exotic, kinky Other to the straight, realist realities of the affluent West.

A proscription such as this, or the position of The Women's Press that they will only look at manuscripts where the protagonist's experience is one with that of the author, raises more questions than it answers. What does the latter policy mean for the Black writer using the novel form— a form developed by the white, European bourgeoisie? And does the Press' position mean automatic exclusion of a manuscript by a Black writer who,

in order to explore racism, develops a white character? If we
accept the argument that the oppressed know more about their
oppressors than the latter about them, and if we accept the fact
that groups like Blacks or Natives are, in the West, essentially
living in a white world, how can we argue that a Black writer's
experience is substantially removed from that of a white character? Surely, as the Kenyan writer Ngugi Wa Thiong'o argues, the
issue is what the Black writer does with the form, and not merely
the origin of the form. But note here how the debate about these
issues once again fails to address the issues and concerns of Black
writers, how the controversy is continually presented in terms of
issues for white writers— a trap the Press neither challenged nor
managed to avoid itself.

This rather tiresomely limited approach, albeit rooted in a
recognition of the appropriation of non-European cultures by
Europeans and North Americans, takes us into very murky
waters and distorts the issue: how to ensure that *all* writers in
Canada have equal access to funding, publication, and to full
reception. What Black writers can benefit from, in my opinion,
is not proscription, such as we have to date, but equal access to
all the resources this society has to offer.

If, however, the debate in the Writers' Union newsletter[4] is
evidence of where writers in Canada are in their thinking on
racism in writing and publishing, then there is every reason to
be pessimistic about the potential for change. With very few
exceptions— all the more noteworthy and noticeable for their
rarity— writers defended their rights and freedoms to use whatever voice they chose to use. I would have hoped that along with
that defence would have been *some* acknowledgment of the
racism endemic to this society, and to the literary arena. It would
have been reassuring if the debate had revealed a wider acknowl-

edgement and understanding of The Women's Press' attempt, flawed as it was, to do something about racism as publishers. The issue of racism, personal, systemic or cosmic has, however, been notably absent from this debate.

Some months later, in the spring of 1989, when presented with the issue, the Writers' Union failed to endorse the setting up of a task force looking into issues of racism in writing and publishing in Canada. This despite significant attempts by a female and feminist minority. The Union *did*, however, pass a motion condemning "the failure of the law of Canada to protect freedom of expression and to prevent far-reaching intrusions into the essential privacy of the writing process." If any proof were needed of my earlier arguments, this tawdry display of white, male privilege provided it; it also confirmed how little interest the Union had in even acknowledging the existence of racism.

The Writers' Union has, to my mind, entirely abdicated its position as an organization that claims to be concerned about the rights of all writers in this country. It is primarily concerned about the rights of white, male writers, and certainly not about Black writers. The Old Boys' Network of Writers would be a far more suitable appellation.

"All art," critic Terry Eagleton writes, "has its roots in social barbarism. Art survives by repressing the historical toil which went into its making, oblivious of its own sordid preconditions... we only know art because we can identify its opposite: labour." There is an evident and appalling failure on the part of white writers to grasp the fact that, despite their relatively low incomes, as a group they are extremely privileged and powerful. There is an accompanying failure to understand how the silencing of the many enables the few to become the articulators and dissemina-tors of knowledge and culture. This is the social barbarism to which Eagleton refers, and it continues today in the erasure of the presence of those others who, by their labour and toil, still help to create art today.

Furthermore, how can white writers insist on their right to use any voice they may choose, and not insist on the equally valid right of African or Native writers to write and to have their work adequately received? How can white writers insist on this right without acknowledging that, on the extremely unlevel playing field that racism creates, the exercise of this right could, in all likelihood, mean that work by a white writer about Natives, for instance, would be more readily received than similar work by a Native writer? To insist on one's right in a political vacuum, as so many writers have, while remaining silent on the equal rights of other writers to be heard, is fundamentally un-democratic and unfair.

The corresponding obligation to the right of these writers to use any voice they may choose to, is first to understand the privilege that has generated the idea that free choice of voice is a right. Second, but more importantly, these writers ought to begin to work to expand the area of that right to include those who, in theory, also have a right to write from any point of view but who, through the practice of racism, have been unable to exercise that right, thereby making it meaningless. Ngugi writes that "the writer as a human being is, himself, a product of history, of time and place."[5] This is what many writers in Canada today have forgotten: that— to continue in the words of Ngugi— they "belong to a certain class" and they are "inevitably... partici-pant(s) in the class struggles of (their) times." I would add to that, the race struggles of their times. These writers have refused even to acknowledge their privilege vis-à-vis their own white working class, let alone Blacks or Natives.

Writers are no more or less racist, classist, or sexist than other individuals. Neither are they any less sensitive to the issue of racism than the average Canadian— which is probably not saying much. Writers ought, however, to recognize and acknowledge that along with their privilege comes a social responsibility. Essentially, the individual writer will decide how to exercise that social responsibility. Writers may, of their own accord, decide not to use the voice of a group their culture has traditionally oppressed. Others may decide that their responsibility impels them to do something else; but they ought to be impelled to do *something*.

Writers coming from a culture that has a history of oppressing the one they wish to write about would do well to examine their motives. Is their interest a continuance of the tradition of oppression, if only in seeing these cultures as different or exotic, as Other? Does their interest come out of the belief that their own cultural material is exhausted, and that just about anything having to do with Africans, Asians and Natives is bound to garner more attention? Is it, perhaps, the outcome of guilt and a desire to make recompense? Such writers have to examine whether they can write without perpetuating stereotypes.

Many readers must be aware of the debacle the English feminist publishing house, Virago, faced when it found that one of its published titles— a collection of short stories about Asians in England— was, in fact, written pseudonymously by a white male— a Church of England minister. It is interesting to note that one of the readers of the manuscript prior to publication, an Asian woman, had drawn attention to the fact that all the girls in the collection of short stories were drawn very passively; the boys, on the other hand, were portrayed as being very aggressive. She actually questioned the authorship of the work, but her suspicions were overridden. We cannot conclude from this that writers from a particular culture would be above pandering to stereotypes about their own culture. For instance, the upper class writer from any culture runs the risk of stereotyping the working class of that culture; however, the chance of stereotypes being portrayed is, in my opinion, far greater with a writer who is, essentially, a stranger to the culture as a whole.

White writers must ask themselves hard questions about these issues; they must understand how their privilege *as white people*, writing *about* another culture, rather than *out of* it virtually guarantees that their work will, in a racist society, be received more readily than the work of writers coming from that very culture. Many of these questions are applicable to all writers: for instance, the Black middle class writer writing about the Black working class; or the upper class Asian writing about the Asian peasant. If, after these questions are asked— and I believe responsible writers must ask them if they wish to be responsible to themselves, their gifts and the larger community— writers still feel impelled to write that story or that novel, then let us hope they are able to "describe a situation so truthfully that the reader can no longer evade." Margaret Laurence accomplished this ideal in her collection of short stories, *The Tomorrow Tamer*; the secret of her accomplishment lies, I believe, in the sense of humility— not traditionally the hallmark of the white person approaching an African, Asian or Native culture— that writers need to bring to the culture to which they are strangers. Writers must be willing to learn; they must be open to having certainties shifted, perhaps permanently. They cannot enter as oppressors, or even as members of the dominant culture. That sense of humility is what has been sorely lacking in the deluge of justifications that have poured forth in support of the "right" of the white writer to use any voice.

While Canadian writers find it very easy to defend the rights of Chinese writers who have been silenced by the state, there is general apathy to the silencing of writers here in Canada through the workings of racism, both within the marketplace and through funding agencies. In an essay titled "The Writer and Responsibility,"[6] South African writer Nadine Gordimer argues that artistic freedom cannot exist without its wider context. She identifies two presences within the writer: creative self-absorption and conscionable awareness. The writer, she says, must resolve "whether these are locked in a death-struggle, or are really foetuses in a twinship of fecundity." For some, artistic freedom appears to be alive and well in Canada; these writers, however, pay not the slightest heed to the fact that the wider context includes many who, because of racism, cannot fully exercise that artistic freedom. In Canada, that wider context is, in fact, very narrowly drawn around the artistic freedom of white writers.

As for the twin presences of creative self-absorption and conscionable awareness which Gordimer identifies, conscionable awareness on any issue but censorship has been disturbingly absent from the debate on the writer and voice. Creative self-absorption, or literary navel-gazing, is what rules the day in Canada.

END NOTES:

1. Sara Maitland, "Triptych," in *A Book of Spells*, Michael Joseph, 1987.

2. Joseph Brodsky, *Less than One*, Viking, 1986.

3. A Puerto Rican painter who is serving a 68 year sentence in state and

federal prisons in the U.S. for seditious conspiracy arising out of his involvement in Puerto Rican liberation struggles.

4. In 1988, the Writers' Union ran a series of letters in its newsletter on the issues of cultural appropriation and the writer and voice. See "Gut Issues in Babylon, Appendix 2," elsewhere in this collection, for further discussion on this issue of the newsletter.

5. Ngugi Wa Thiong'o, "Writers in Politics," in *Kenyan Culture: The National Struggle for Survival*.

6. Nadine Gordimer, *The Essential Gesture: Writing, Politics and Places*, London: Penguin, 1988.